FINDING A PLACE TO STAND

FINDING A PLACE TO STAND
Developing Self-Reflective Institutions, Leaders and Citizens

Edward R. Shapiro

PHOENIX
PUBLISHING HOUSE
firing the mind

First published in 2020 by
Phoenix Publishing House Ltd
62 Bucknell Road
Bicester
Oxfordshire OX26 2DS

Copyright © 2020 by Edward R. Shapiro

The right of Edward R. Shapiro to be identified as the author of this work has been asserted in accordance with §§ 77 and 78 of the Copyright Design and Patents Act 1988.

All rights reserved. No part of this publication may be reproduced, stored in a retrieval system, or transmitted, in any form or by any means, electronic, mechanical, photocopying, recording, or otherwise, without the prior written permission of the publisher.

British Library Cataloguing in Publication Data

A C.I.P. for this book is available from the British Library

ISBN-13: 978-1-912691-33-3

Typeset by Medlar Publishing Solutions Pvt Ltd, India

Printed in the United Kingdom

www.firingthemind.com

*For
Donna Elmendorf*

How are they right?

"Very shortly, you will be going onto your assigned wards. Within those wards, you will see over fifty of the sickest, craziest, most bizarre people you will ever encounter. They will be hallucinating, gesticulating, and delusional in the most grotesque ways. Every cell in your body will rebel and want to block out the experience. But here is the thing you must remember. Every one of those symptoms, as strange as they may seem to you, makes perfect sense to those people. Every single one, has been evolved and carefully crafted, to try to deal with some impossible family situation. Every symptom represents an attempt by that person to adapt to the hand that fate has dealt him. You are to regard each one as an artistic, creative endeavor to survive. Your job, and your only job, is to appreciate, and admire that effort!"

—Elvin Semrad, MD, welcoming new psychiatric residents to Massachusetts Mental Health Center, circa 1968

Contents

Permissions ix
Acknowledgments xi
About the author xv
Foreword xvii

Part I: Joining

CHAPTER ONE
How Are They Right? 3

CHAPTER TWO
Containment and Communication 11

CHAPTER THREE
Making Sense of Organizational Dynamics 19

CHAPTER FOUR
The Interpretive Stance 27

CHAPTER FIVE
Taking Up a Role: A Case Example 37

Part II: Leadership and the Self-reflective Institution

CHAPTER SIX
The CEO: Grappling with Systems Pressures — 49

CHAPTER SEVEN
Learning about Systems Psychodynamics:
The Group Relations Conference — 59

CHAPTER EIGHT
From Group Relations to Leadership — 69

CHAPTER NINE
Shaping a Mission: A Case Example — 81

CHAPTER TEN
A Citizenship Laboratory — 97

CHAPTER ELEVEN
Derailment and Recalibration of the Mission — 109

Part III: A Citizen in Society

CHAPTER TWELVE
Approaching Society through Institutions — 123

CHAPTER THIRTEEN
Do Nations Have Missions? American Identity — 135

CHAPTER FOURTEEN
Citizenship as Development — 147

CHAPTER FIFTEEN
Society as a Multicellular Learning System — 157

Conclusion — 163
References — 167
Index — 175

Permissions

The following chapters have been adapted with permission from the sources indicated:

Parts of the Foreword appeared in Shapiro, E. R. (2000). The individual in context. In: J. J. Shay & J. Wheelis (Eds.), *Psychotherapy* (pp. 337–358). New York: Ardent Media.

Chapter 1: Shapiro, E. R. (2005). Joining a group's task: the discovery of hope and respect. *International Journal of Group Psychotherapy*, 55(2): 211–217.

Chapter 2: Shapiro, E. R. (1982). The holding environment and family therapy with acting out adolescents. *International Journal of Psychoanalytic Psychotherapy*, 9: 209–226.

Shapiro, E. R. (2012). Management vs interpretation: Teaching residents to listen. *Journal of Nervous and Mental Disease*, 200(3): 204–207.

Chapters 3 and 4: Shapiro, E. R., & Carr, A. W. (1991). The interpretive stance. In: *Lost in Familiar Places: Creating New Connections between the Individual and Society* (pp. 75–87). New Haven, CT: Yale University Press.

Chapter 5: Shapiro, E. R., & Carr. A. W. (1991). An organizational illustration. In: *Lost in Familiar Places: Creating New Connections between the Individual and Society* (pp. 88–94). New Haven, CT: Yale University Press.

Chapter 6: Shapiro, E. R. (2001). The changing role of the CEO. *Organisational and Social Dynamics*, 1(1): 130–142.

Chapter 7: Shapiro, E. R., & Carr, A. W. (2012). An introduction to Tavistock Style Group Relations Conference Learning. *Organisational and Social Dynamics*, *12*(1): 70–80.

Chapter 8: Shapiro, E. R. (2017). Learning from the director's role: Leadership and vulnerability. *Organisational and Social Dynamics*, *16*(2): 255–270.

Chapter 9: Shapiro, E. R. (2001). Institutional learning as chief executive. In: L. J. Gould, L. F. Stapley, & M. Stein (Eds.), *The Systems Psychodynamics of Organizations: Integrating the Group Relations Approach, Psychoanalytic, and Open Systems Theory* (pp. 175–195). New York: Karnac.

Chapter 10: Shapiro, E. R. (2009). A view from Riggs: Treatment resistance and patient authority, XII: Examined living: A psychodynamic treatment system. *Journal of the American Academy of Psychoanalysis*, *37*(4): 683–698. Reprinted with permission of Guilford Press.

Chapter 11: Shapiro, E. R. (2013). Derailment in organizational development: Consultations to the Austen Riggs Center. *Organisational and Social Dynamics*, *13*(1): 41–54.

Chapter 12: Shapiro, E. R., & Carr, A. W. (2006). "These people were some kind of solution": can society in any sense be understood? *Organisational and Social Dynamics*, *6*(2): 241–257.

Shapiro, E. R. (2019). Wesley Carr, religious institutions and institutional integrity. *Organisational and Social Dynamics, 19*(1): 103–111.

Chapter 13: Shapiro, E. R. (2013). The maturation of American identity: A study of the elections of 1996 and 2000 and the war against terrorism. *Organisational and Social Dynamics*, *3*(1): 121–133.

Chapter 14: Shapiro, E. R., & Carr, A. W. (2017). Citizenship as development. *Organisational and Social Dynamics*, *17*(2): 278–288.

Acknowledgments

The fact that this book is to be published the same year that the Austen Riggs Center celebrates its 100th anniversary and the A. K. Rice Institute (AKRI) celebrates its 50th is a moving coincidence for me. As the reader will see, these two institutions have helped me to form the central ideas developed in these pages. Both have held firm to their missions for generations, focusing on the impact of the social context on the individual. I am very grateful to the staff and patients at Riggs and the generations of men and women who have attended group relations conferences organized by AKRI for their contributions to the development of systems psychodynamics. Central figures in the group relations world who have helped me to learn are Margaret Rioch, Roger Shapiro, Kathleen Pogue White, Larry Gould, Shmuel Erlich, Mira Erlich-Ginor, Wesley Carr, Leroy Wells, and Jim Krantz. Jim, who was a member with me in a training group with Margaret Rioch, has become a lifelong friend, walking with me through every insight, consulting to my organizations, and joining my family. His love of this work has been unflaggingly sustaining.

The book represents a lifetime of learning from others; I have a lot of people to thank. When I was an undergraduate at Yale, Denis Mickiewicz directed the Yale Russian Chorus. My many trips to the Soviet Union during the Cold War with that group, beginning when I was nineteen, had us singing on street corners and talking with Soviet citizens until the early mornings. Denis' passion for democracy and his management of this group of undergraduate and graduate students under intense and dangerous circumstances in a foreign context taught me about joining a mission and the risky commitment involved in standing up for what matters.

The Russell Sage and Ford Foundations supported my anthropology studies and fieldwork in the hills and fishing villages of Tobago, West Indies. I was a solitary white medical student studying native medicine; Cliff Barnett, who led the medical-anthropology program at Stanford, taught me participant-observation and how to claim a workable role in a foreign culture.

Elvin Semrad, whose quote opens the book, taught me how to listen. I identified with the amazing way his capacity to listen to psychiatric patients helped transform what seemed terrifying and overwhelming into what was normal human pain and understandable (Semrad, 1969). Roger Shapiro introduced me to a way of listening to families; his perspective on family treatment taught me how groups work together and how an interpretive intervention can lead to a deeper and collective understanding. My National Institute of Mental Health (NIMH) work group with Roger, John Zinner, and David Berkowitz taught me how to write from experience. David Reiss, who led the Adult Psychiatry Branch of NIMH when I was there, encouraged me to take the risk to have ideas and present them in public.

Shervert Frazier hired me at McLean Hospital and gave me, as a very young man, the extraordinary opportunity to build a new and untested program for adolescents and families in a venerable institution. His steady support and confidence opened doors for new learning. I began my program at McLean with Jonathan Kolb, whose clear thinking and integrity helped our program become established and led to a cherished friendship. John Nemiah, then the editor of the *American Journal of Psychiatry*, encouraged me to think through and articulate the contextual aspects of personality development (E. R. Shapiro, 1978b).

John Maynard and Betty Kramer, as chairman and president of the Austen Riggs Center board, hired me as the medical director. Their mentorship and support were the beginnings of sustaining collaboration with a series of board chairs at Riggs, including Mary Carswell, Philip Winterer, Mason Smith, and Lisa Raskin. They headed a diverse and dedicated group of trustees whose wise advice helped me to lead. Aso Tavitian, the vice-chair of the board, generously opened his home and his mind to help me and Riggs through difficult times. Dwight Jewson, who joined the board at Riggs from the world of marketing, helped us to frame our institutional mission and became a close friend. My thinking about the links between institutions and the larger society has been shaped by his work. During my time at Riggs, Jerry Fromm, John Muller, Jim Sacksteder, Eric Plakun, and Jane Tillman helped me to hold the institution together through chaotic changes in the outside world.

Wesley Carr, through his experience in the Church of England, brought me out of the consulting room and into the world. Our decades of collaboration and friendship illuminated for me how vastly differentiated capacities, backgrounds, and national perspectives might be brought together for negotiated understanding around a shared task.

Ileene Smith helped me to think through the publication of this book. She pointed me toward John Knight, who helped me to shape the first draft. John's ability to see through the range of ideas I was struggling with to a shape that began to make sense was enormously helpful. Susan Long's generous perspective helped clarify my tone and approach.

My family has supported and allowed this work to unfold. My three boys, Josh, Zach, and Jake—now men—taught me about families and development in ways that have transformed my understanding. I am more grateful to them for teaching me about fatherhood, for challenging me, for becoming the men they are, and for putting up with me than I can ever say in words.

But this book is dedicated to the woman who is everything to me: my wife, partner, colleague, best friend, and the love of my life, Donna Elmendorf. Donna's generosity, sensitivity, and deep capacity for love, combined with her focused attention to the needs and vulnerabilities of others, her tough-minded insistence on truth and integrity, her rigorous editing of my style and ideas, and her clear commitment to the primary task of our family and of every institution she has worked in have helped create a family world where our children and I are free to be who we are. She is the source and the outcome. I dedicate this book to her with profound gratitude and love.

About the author

Edward R. Shapiro, MD, was the medical director/CEO of the Austen Riggs Center from 1991 to 2011. A board-certified psychiatrist, psychoanalyst, family researcher, and organizational consultant, he is also clinical professor of psychiatry at Yale University School of Medicine and principal of the Boswell Group. He is on the boards of the A. K. Rice Institute and the International Dialogue Initiative, and on the advisory board of Partners Confronting Collective Atrocities. A founding member of the Psychoanalytic Society and Institute of the Berkshires, Dr. Shapiro is a training and supervising analyst. An organizational consultant for over forty years, Dr. Shapiro has consulted with hospitals, mental health clinics, law firms, and family businesses. He has published more than fifty articles and book chapters on human and organizational development, family functioning, and personality disorders, presenting papers in the United States and abroad. His book (with A. W. Carr), *Lost in Familiar Places: Creating New Connections between the Individual and Society*, was published by Yale University Press as was his edited book, *The Inner World in the Outer World: Psychoanalytic Perspectives*. A Distinguished Life Fellow of the American Psychiatric Association, he is also a Fellow of the A. K. Rice Institute and the American College of Psychoanalysis. Dr. Shapiro has received the Felix and Helene Deutsch Scientific Award from the Boston Psychoanalytic Society, the Research Prize from the Society for Family Therapy and Research, and the Philip Isenberg Teaching Award from McLean Hospital. In 2007, he was named Outstanding Psychiatrist for Advancement of the Profession by the Massachusetts Psychiatric Association and since 2011 has been on US News & World Report's list of "Top Doctors."

FOREWORD

The Evolution of an Idea

This book traces a psychological pathway from family membership to joining society as a citizen. I have written it because of the unusual opportunities I have had to learn that our institutions, our access to society, have untapped capacities to help us develop our citizen voices. Using my experience in a range of roles and settings from psychoanalysis to family treatment, from group relations to studying voters, from institutional membership to the leadership of a unique psychodynamic hospital, I will attempt to demonstrate how focused attention on our experiences in roles, an understanding of systems psychodynamics, and a reorientation of our institutional leaders can help bring us out into the world with clearer perspectives as citizens.

Facing the swirl of global, technological, and political transformation and the correspondingly weakened citizen voice, I have been struck by the difficulty of finding a place to stand with others and speak with any clarity about things that actually matter. Society is too vast for any of us as individuals to see much more than our projections into it. Can we perceive more if we find a way to look at society collaboratively? Is there any way to clarify the psychological steps toward becoming a citizen? And if so, what is the appropriate context?

The family is the organizational context within which we develop. The family contains and represents certain standards and carries out on behalf of the larger society the task of producing mature adults. Family membership is our first involvement in an organization and becomes the model for our engagement in the myriad organizations which constitute the world. Once we leave the family as adults, there is psychological work involved in joining groups and organizations as members, but the framework of roles and tasks is similar. Claiming the citizen role, however—determining who the other members are of such a system, discovering links with them, and discerning and joining the tasks of the larger society—stretches our capacities.

In the last century, our increasing ability to communicate with one another has meant that negotiating a social role that begins in the family, moves to various organizations, and reaches into the larger society has required us to begin to conceptualize something called "the global citizen." We have yet to define the particulars of this role—what it entails morally, politically, and personally—in part because the context of our global tasks is so vast as to be almost incomprehensible. However, in the absence of our finding a place to stand and speak with authority as citizens about things that matter, we run the risk of abandoning society to authoritarian leaders who fragment humanity into nationalistic subgroups or escalate the irrationalities inherent in large groups. How can we begin to understand the internal and external pressures that might mold us into developing citizens who can take the risk of having a social voice?

I have been working for most of my career on the study of the individual in context, focusing on the confluence of internal psychological pressures with external social demands, and the way that managing these pressures can move people toward engagement with the larger society. I have had unusual opportunities to study the unconscious functioning of individuals, families, and organizations as a psychoanalyst, a family and group dynamics researcher, and an organizational leader. In 1991, I coauthored a book with the late Dean of Westminster, Wesley Carr, outlining an approach to the study of collective irrationality (E. R. Shapiro & Carr, 1991). Focusing on families and on institutions such as Westminster Abbey and the Harvard-affiliated psychiatric institution, McLean Hospital, we formulated an interpretive stance where individuals can begin to make sense of their experience through a recognition of differentiated roles within a shared context. This book takes the argument a step further, focusing on the psychology of citizenship, the potential for discovering a voice, and a model for our developing society.

Psychoanalytic training and family process

In my early years of psychiatric training, I was appointed to the Public Health Service during the Vietnam War and assigned to the Adult Psychiatry Branch of the National Institute of Mental Health (NIMH). At the time, Roger Shapiro (no relation) and John Zinner were studying the relationship between family experience and personality development in adolescents (Scharff, 1989; R. L. Shapiro, 1966; R. L. Shapiro & Zinner, 1976; Zinner & R. L. Shapiro, 1972, 1974). Roger and John were both psychoanalysts working in an unusual clinical research setting where families fully participated in their adolescent's treatment and agreed to have their intensive psychodynamic treatment studied. In their writings about this work, Shapiro and Zinner illuminated a way to hold onto psychoanalytic theory and an interpretive tradition while moving outside of the boundaries of the individual. They amended the concept of projective identification, first introduced by Melanie Klein (1946) and further developed by Otto Kernberg (1966, 1975, 1976), as an internal psychological mechanism shaping how individuals manage relationships in their minds. They recognized that projective identification is an interpersonal defense in families where individuals identify aspects of themselves as "good" and project what they consider "bad" onto others while maintaining an unconscious link to those projections (Zinner & R. L. Shapiro, 1972). They could demonstrate how the entire family group participates in this defense; it shapes family members' developmental course (Zinner & R. L. Shapiro, 1974). This formulation allowed a deeper examination of the feelings that develop in all group relationships in relation to particular tasks.

Roger and John used the work of Erik Erikson (1950, 1956, 1958a, 1968) and Wilfred Bion (1961, 1977) in developing their ideas. Through my work with them, I became a student of Erikson's writing on adolescent identity and Bion's work on group dynamics. Erikson had articulated the concept of mutuality, underlining the crucial coordination between the developing individual and his human (social) environment. He recognized that identity represents the increasing confluence of the individual's views of the self and the views of that self, coming from others. Erikson defined integrity as our obligation to the most mature meaning available to us, illuminating how we are inextricably bound to sociocultural and historical forces. He suggested that integrity required the discovery of larger social tasks to which the individual can become committed (E. R. Shapiro & Fromm, 1999).

Bion, too, recognized social connectedness; his initial work focused on the small work group. He appreciated that we are always embedded in groups and articulated the links between our conscious commitment to a group's task and other less conscious behavior that can take us over in these settings. His recognition of the shared unconscious forces that can sway group functioning opened a new way to consider some of the problems of social engagement.

One aspect of the research at NIMH was clinical, treating troubled adolescents in intensive individual and family therapy in front of a one-way mirror in order to study the relationship between family experience and individual disturbance. At one point, I was working with a young girl in a family where the father's fragile self-esteem was maintained by an unconscious family agreement to see him as only good, generous, and responsive. This is a classic example of an irrational perception and it carried with it the consequent projection of all that was "bad" onto another family member, in this case my adolescent patient. Neither the girl nor her father could be perceived by the family in all their human complexity.

In one family meeting, the parents and siblings insisted that my patient's perceptions about her father's unavailability could not possibly be true. She was experiencing him as insensitive, but the family could not conceive of him as ever being bad in that way. My patient had a choice. She could agree with her family and give up her experience, allowing her to join with and be accepted in this little organization thereby affirming and adopting these irrational roles (the "good (sensitive) father" and the "bad (blaming) adolescent"). Or, she could insist on her own perspective and suffer rejection.

In an individual therapy meeting after the family meeting I found myself replicating the family dynamic in astonishing detail by challenging my patient's experience. She had angrily accused me of excluding her visitors and I had responded defensively by accusing her of distorting reality. Her explosive reaction stunned me. Unwittingly, I was asking her to preserve an idealized view of me just as her family had done with her father. Remembering the earlier family session allowed me to gain perspective on the repetition, my patient's powerful reaction, and my unwitting contribution.

The day I grasped this uncanny repetition, I realized what I wanted to do with my career. I needed to learn something about human systems. For reasons I could not understand, I had suddenly joined an irrational system that carried and had enacted a developmental past. The extended group irrationality we all had entered into required an additional perspective. I was learning how a family could function as an irrational group and hinder the development of family members. I saw how unconscious collusion could fit the developmental dynamics of each individual and contribute to a group regression that turned out to be characteristic of earlier periods in the family's life.

Working with the NIMH group, I began to conceptualize the family's task as helping each individual (parent and child) master the relevant developmental stage. I could see how easy it was for the family as a social organization to lose touch with its task when it gets caught in the immediate pressures of individual experience. I recognized the value to the struggling family of an observer who could manage to hold and articulate an outside perspective, allowing the family group and each member to grasp their regression and join with other family members in more task-related work. But I also came to understand how an outsider could get caught up in this shared irrationality. I began to discern how the unconscious pressures that were pulling family members away from the family's developmental task came both from inside (parental histories, or transgenerational conflict) and outside (the pressures from living in the world) of the family organization (Berkowitz et al., 1974a, 1974b; E. R. Shapiro et al., 1975; E. R. Shapiro et al., 1977; Zinner & E. R. Shapiro, 1975).

McLean Hospital and Tavistock Group Relations

When the psychodynamic research unit at NIMH closed in 1974, I returned to Boston and founded the Adolescent and Family Treatment and Study Center at McLean Hospital, a program that I directed for fifteen years. While I completed my psychoanalytic training, my program developed a psychodynamic clinical approach for severely disturbed adolescents and families in an open setting, derived from my NIMH research (E. R. Shapiro, 1978a, 1978b, 1982a, 1982b; E. R. Shapiro & Carr, 1987; E. R. Shapiro & Freedman, 1987; E. R. Shapiro & Kolb, 1979).

McLean gave me my first experience of being an administrator. I was the program director and was therefore faced with the difficulties of managing a multidisciplinary group in relation to the larger organization. My NIMH mentor, Roger Shapiro, had for years been directing experiential conferences in what is known as the Tavistock tradition. In this method, a group of diverse individuals gathers over several days in a residential setting to create an organization in order to study its dynamics (see Chapter Seven). I signed up as a member of a conference and began a second period of intense learning.

In the relatively unstructured atmosphere of an experiential conference on leadership and authority, I found myself unwittingly constructing a group with the same dynamics as the one I was developing at McLean. I could see the ways in which my own personality contributed to the group's difficulties. My perfectionism in the leadership role had stifled the group's creativity and my narcissism had obscured the contributions of outside groups. As in my learning at NIMH, I was again stunned by the way in which the dynamics of projective identification recreated and illuminated group, individual, and system-wide phenomena. I saw how my own character evoked projections from others in my group that shaped the ways we were all able to work. My speaking with what looked like certainty led others to depend on me so that they hesitated to bring in their own ideas. I began to recognize the links between my family role and my organizational role and found the experience as stimulating and powerful as my own psychoanalysis.

Over the next four decades, I served both as staff member and director of more than forty experiential group relations conferences in the United States and Europe. I also began to develop a private practice as an organizational consultant, working with hospitals, law firms, and family businesses. I was deepening my recognition that the boundary around the individual was more permeable than I had been taught. The inner world and the outer world were in dynamic interaction; I began to understand Bion's recognition that we are always embedded in groups (E. R. Shapiro, 1985, 1997a, 1997b).

In 1980, I served on the staff at one of the group relations conferences with Wesley Carr, then a young English cleric. He had developed an understanding of organizations through the Tavistock Institute for Human Relations in London. We struck up a friendship and found a connection between his understanding of the larger social meaning of institutions (through his work in the Church of England) and my grasp of the individual's development in the family. Our book, *Lost in Familiar Places* (E. R. Shapiro & Carr, 1991), began to articulate a methodology for interpreting irrationality in organizational life, recognizing the effect of the social context on individual development and functioning. We formulated an approach for grasping the dynamics of an institution through listening for how the other is right and trying to make sense of the connections. The contribution of Wesley's thinking is evident throughout this book, particularly in Chapters Three, Four, Five, Seven, Twelve, and Fourteen, which are adaptations of work we developed together prior to his death.

The Austen Riggs Center

The Austen Riggs Center is a psychodynamic hospital and residential treatment center in Stockbridge, Massachusetts. I became interested in the center in 1985 while I was still at work in Boston doing intensive treatment with troubled adolescents and families. Looking for other institutions committed to a depth psychological approach with inpatients, I learned about Riggs' long and venerated psychoanalytic past and its traditions of providing intensive psychotherapy in a completely open setting. Austen Riggs Center had been the professional home for Erik Erikson; he had written *Young Man Luther*, using the case of a patient at Riggs as a stimulus for his ideas of social connection and commitment (Erikson, 1958a, 1958b; E. R. Shapiro & Fromm, 1999). In 1991, while looking for an opportunity to apply my developing ideas from the top down in an organization, I was lucky enough to become the next medical director and CEO of the center.

The open setting at Riggs is central to its treatment philosophy. The center gives the most troubled patients, some coming from locked wards and seclusion rooms, the freedom to come and go, bringing them face to face with their ultimate responsibility for their own lives—in a therapeutic community of examined living. At Riggs, patients take up many roles: patient, student, and citizen of the Riggs community. Their struggles to find their active citizenship in this setting in relation to their own psychological development and treatment are illuminating (see Chapter Ten).

In my twenty years as medical director/CEO at Riggs, we brought families fully into the center's treatment design and developed a contextual focus for the treatment (E. R. Shapiro, 1997a, 1997b, 2004, 2005, 2009). Our mission became "the study and treatment of the individual in context." During this time, I strove to combine Riggs' focus on patient authority with my growing sense of social connectivity. Not only was I responsible for how the organization was working but I began to consider what responsibility this organization had to the larger political world. Were we engaged in work that mattered beyond our institution? With the tumultuous events of the early twenty-first century, I found myself increasingly compelled to turn my clinical approach outward and focus my attention on a study of citizenship and the social dynamics of the larger society.

Initially convinced that a relatively neutral analyst could deeply grasp some of the secrets of the individual's unconscious, I had gradually learned how the personality of the observer influenced the data. From there, it became easier to examine the next series of bounded contexts: the couple, the family, the group, the organization, and society. Now, when I see individuals in treatment, particularly the more disturbed and traumatized ones, I also see the impact of the outside world. Understanding the context does not replace understanding the individual; broadening the focus allows a more comprehensive understanding of both. For example, when I see a patient who is dissociating, unable to integrate herself and communicating her distress through her behavior, I frequently see more than her internal conflicts. I begin to hear about the divorced, angry parental marriage that she internalized, the generations of conflict and trauma behind those parents, the treatment systems that worked with the patient, parents, and resources without talking to each other, and the pressures of rapid social change and resulting lack of reflective spaces.

In 1996, I was invited to participate in a nationwide study of unaffiliated voters by the Center for National Policy in Washington, DC. The opportunity for extended individual interviews with a diverse group of citizens in combination with my group relations work and the intense involvement with citizen-patients at Riggs gave me the chance to combine my clinical work with a deeper consideration of the role of the citizen (E. R. Shapiro, 2000a, 2000b, 2003). I began to consider how—through our roles as members of groups and institutions—we might gain a useful perspective on the seemingly irrational forces that impact our lives. This book suggests that with this perspective we might be better able to engage with our world as citizens in order more effectively to take charge of what is happening to us.

Part I

Joining

Becoming a participating citizen and having a public voice requires an ability to discover connections between people through shared membership. Joining a group exposes us to group dynamics, the management of irrationality, and the discovery of larger social connections. Taking our role-related experience seriously and trying to make sense of it is an initial step toward social interpretation and the development of a citizen voice.

We (most of us) begin life as members of a family organization; we take up a role in relation to the family's developmental task. In this section of the book, I focus on a way of listening to others, the unconscious elements of the joining process, the transition from family membership to group membership, the relationship of organizational role to the organization's mission, and the ways in which groups and organizations can begin to contain intense emotions and use them in the service of their tasks.

In Chapter Four, I offer a case study where my efforts to take seriously my experience in an assigned organizational role began to make sense of an organization's collective functioning. The case demonstrates how learning to negotiate with others a shared understanding of a group's process can contribute to the possibility of speaking on its behalf, a central aspect of effective citizenship.

CHAPTER ONE

How Are They Right?

Citizenship is not just a legal status. It defines a membership role in a group with a social task and purpose. Becoming a member and developing a representative voice requires a joining process that has a developmental history. We learn the role of member from the beginning in our family; membership is our birthright. We learn the structure of rules, values, and roles that encompass family membership. The psychological boundary that begins to shape each of us as unique individuals has its origins there. As we join groups outside of the family and get invested in identifying with the other people, we relax that individual boundary. This process begins a transformation from "*me as an individual*" toward "*me as a member*" and begins to allow me to see other people not as "*the other*" but as "*one of us.*" Once outside of the family, peer group dynamics of inclusion and exclusion further shape our sense of ourselves. We choose and are chosen to be a member for reasons that initially are beyond our grasp. But we learn from this process and, increasingly, we take charge of our decisions to join.

Joining a group requires the capacity to identify with the group's task and link our ideas to what others are saying. Affirming the other's perspective and searching creatively for a larger context that links differing views are initial steps toward membership. To do that, we must first consider "How are they right," that is, *what aspect of what they are saying fits with my experience*? I will present three stories about joining, each describing an individual's discovery of a bridging connection that offered an opportunity for overcoming isolation by revealing a shared and larger context.

Philadelphia

The first story is a small example of joining. It comes from a visit my colleagues and I made to a reception in Philadelphia for the Austen Riggs Center, where we met with a group of clinicians to talk about our work. A number of senior clinicians attended this gathering because of a wish to hear more about Riggs and think through the implications of our work with treatment-resistant patients for their practices. As with many clinicians who work with difficult cases in outpatient treatment, these doctors were grateful for Riggs' survival in the managed-care climate, which was limiting the financial resources available for treatment. Riggs had a long tradition of commitment to an intensive psychotherapeutic approach that seemed increasingly to be facing external institutional attacks on its survival. The meeting was organized both to support these outside clinicians who worked psychodynamically with severely troubled patients and to add them to Riggs' referral base.

After receiving a brief presentation of the institution and an outline of our clinical approach, people began describing their practices and the struggles they were having with hard-to-treat patients. After several had spoken, a very senior clinician said, "I've always thought my practice was stimulating until a year ago when I had an epiphany." He then described how he was sitting at a dinner party and, looking across the table, he saw a spoon begin to curl up in front of him. He then saw other items in the room begin to move by themselves, some out through the door to the outside garden. He detailed his unfolding excitement about people's ability to do miraculous things if they only believed, describing how one person could levitate a heavier person with just two fingers under the arms if they believed deeply enough!

People in the room were hushed and tense as he elaborated this. My colleagues and I were stunned, thinking about how to manage this unexpected and seemingly irrational presentation in the context of this elegant and clinically focused reception. Some of the clinicians, trying to be supportive and contain their skepticism and concern, spoke of their knowledge about parapsychology and experiments with mind control of inanimate objects. Their comments spurred the speaker on to more extravagant descriptions about the power of belief. The discussion was being shaped in an unpredicted way that appeared to be taking us far away from the problems of treatment-resistant patients. Finally, I intervened: "I know just what you mean about the power of belief," I said. "Many clinicians have told me that they just could not believe that any institution devoted to psychodynamic treatment could survive in this healthcare world." This oblique but task-related comment brought relieved laughter from the group, and the discussion easily turned back to the shared focus around treatment.

As I thought about this later, I wondered if this elderly man's comments were stimulated by his anxiety about his own survival. I realized that his taking up a seemingly irrational role, presenting divergent comments about the power of belief, could potentially be understood as connected to the group's anxiety about our evening's theme. In this context, my effort to link his comments to the survival of Riggs allowed the group to place our shared anxiety in perspective, rejoin the issue under discussion, and strengthen the boundary around the group, bringing the elderly clinician back into a more rational and task-related conversation.

This is a simple story about bringing in a shared context to reintegrate an isolating and isolated group member. But the question it raised for me is about what it takes to listen respectfully to the most manifestly irrational and seemingly off-base comment so as to discern how it might be right and connected. It would have been easy to listen to this man's comments as nonsensical and disregard them and, by extension, him. But that kind of judgmental and disrespectful listening would inevitably have furthered his isolation and heightened our anxiety, while reassuring us that at least we weren't irrational. Finding a way to join a shared context was difficult but not impossible (Carr & E. R. Shapiro, 1989).

The piano

My second story is a bit more complex. It occurred at the Austen Riggs Center when I was coming in as the new medical director and CEO. Riggs is a completely open setting that offers a spectrum of care for treatment-resistant patients. In an effort to maximally authorize patients' competence, the center authorizes the patients' complete freedom to come and go, with no restrictions or privilege systems. In addition to intensive psychotherapy, psychopharmacology, and family work, patients participate in an active therapeutic community where, through elected office, they govern themselves and participate in the management of the center's community life.

In negotiating the details of the medical director's residence, I had inquired of the administration about a piano. Prior to my arrival, the retiring medical director had decided with the trustees that the patients were not using all of their five pianos and that one of them could easily be relocated into the medical director's home for social events. During the transition, the hospital community was in some disarray around the management of resources. Consequently, no effective discussion about the piano was carried out with the patients or with me prior to my arrival.

As a result, the patients greeted me with outrage that I had "stolen" their piano. Even though they were not using the piano, they were adamant that it "belonged" to them. In their experience, I was the CEO with all my perks, and they were the abused victims of forceful power. As I saw it, some sort of negotiation had occurred before I arrived, and they were reacting to it in a way I could not grasp; I felt equally victimized and righteous.

So, the patients and I met—forty of them and me. We attempted to negotiate a shared reality with frustrations on all sides. The discussion focused on power—who controlled the pianos, the patients or the medical director? There was no possibility of neutral ground. On the face of it, the question seemed perplexing since pianos were a resource of the institution and I was in charge of resources. To take up the authority of my role required me to link available resources to the institution's task. At this moment, however, asserting that role in the face of the patients' concerns would have been simply a power operation since I could not discover with them the shared task that the resources needed to join. Without understanding what we were involved in, I could not act; we were stuck. I tried to listen to how they were right but could not find the appropriate context.

But then one patient spoke movingly of the terrible sense of helplessness she had felt when the piano was arbitrarily moved without her consent. Though she did not play the piano and knew that other patients didn't use it, she felt strongly that something terribly important had been taken away. From the perspective of the treatment context at Riggs, this made sense. The patients were willingly participating in a clinical situation where, as citizens of a therapeutic community, they had autonomy over their treatment. When the piano was taken from them without their input, they were feeling as though the institution had seemingly betrayed their trust and by extension compromised the negotiated task of restoring them to health.

Even though this perspective was understandable, it was not opening a solution. The patients' passion and the language of helplessness, however, suddenly seemed to open up a larger context beyond the institution.

With a barely perceptible shift, we suddenly found ourselves talking about money, insurance, third-party payers, and managed care. The patients had entered the hospital and begun their engagement in treatment when suddenly, without their participation, their financial resources were arbitrarily and irrevocably ripped away. The piano suddenly became less important as we discovered a larger context for this discussion. We were talking about the task of treatment and the resources for providing it. I could join them, not by projecting negative images about power into managed-care companies, but by working with them on the feelings of helplessness and vulnerability they had about the encroachments of reality and limited resources; these were feelings I also had in my leadership role. In fact, some of these feelings had contributed to my anxious wish to provide a formal space in my home to bring in outsiders and raise money for the hospital.

When we returned to the piano, the patients and I discovered that we could negotiate a process for its review, discussion, and decision. In the context of the shared treatment task, we had uncovered through our various roles a mutual experience of relative helplessness in the face of limited resources. Perhaps one of the functions of a discovered shared context is to provide a resting place that allows a beginning integration of what might initially seem to be competing experiences. The patients were regressively experiencing a repetition of unempathic, arbitrary power; I was in a similar regression of feeling misunderstood by them. In this mutual experience of empathic failure, both sides felt hurt, abused, and unable to learn from each other. Our discovery of the shared task allowed us all to recognize our connections as members of this institution, recover from the mutual regression, and join in an interpretation of a shared reality that we were all grappling with from different roles in a community that we all cared about.

But how could I be sure that my interest in the metaphor of limited resources and the apparently shared context of the third-party payers was not simply self-serving and designed to allow me to mask my own arbitrariness and facilitate my keeping the piano? The patients and I together represented a system in enormous flux, both inside and outside of the hospital. It may have been too much to expect to hold onto a shared context long enough to negotiate a meaningful picture of the significance of the piano without the rest of the system. Though I did keep the piano in my home and arranged to have the pianos in the patient community retuned and reconditioned, we did not revisit this issue after that powerful discussion.

But the evidence that we had found at least the beginnings of a real negotiation came five months later. The patients left me a Christmas stocking on my office door. Inside the stocking were two offerings: a lump of coal and a beautiful, tiny wooden piano, with a tag that said, "This one's on us!"

The bus ride

My third story comes from a British conference I attended. Tom, a social worker of West Indian descent and a member of an Anglican church, reported the following: "I was on a bus during the firemen's strike and a group of black teenagers began harassing the white bus driver. None of the other passengers, who were all white, moved or intervened in any way. As the teenagers' harassment grew in intensity, I thought with some irritation and anxiety, 'Why do I have to do this?' Finally, I got up and spoke to the kids about the current tensions in the environment and the dangers of their behavior and asked them to knock it off, which they did. I did not like the role I was in."

The firemen's strike took place in London and had evoked significant social anxiety, opening vulnerability and dependency and stimulating anger and blame between segments of the population. Emergency crews were threatened during the brief strike; tensions were running high and these were reflected on the bus. Tom's response concisely conveys many of the dilemmas of joining raised by the two earlier stories, but this time the solution is not asserted (as I did in the first story) or discovered (as the patients and I did together in the second). Here the solution is almost forced upon Tom by a complex set of internal and external pressures. The dynamics of the total event move us beyond the small group to consider immersion in the multiple subgroupings of our larger society.

In this event, Tom initially found himself alone. Then he felt himself, almost against his will, in a role. He felt pulled in ways he couldn't fully articulate or discern into a risky engagement with others and with a task that transcended his personal needs. Tom asked himself, poignantly, "Why do I have to do this?" which raises a number of questions. Who says he "has to"? Are the pressures he experiences coming from his personal psychology or from the social surround? What internalized group is he joining, why, and through what process? And, for whom is he responding?

Tom's question, "Why do I have to do this?" can be translated as: "What groups and roles do I represent?" Answer: black man, father, social worker, church member, British citizen. And, from that range of identities, "What do I feel moved to do in this particular group and why?"

Tom's second comment is similarly puzzling. He says, "I did not like the role I was in." What is the nature of this role, and does he mean that this role does not feel like a part of him? How can such a thing happen?

The more we become aware that our experience of ourselves is affected by others, not just in our families but in the larger contexts in which we live, the less sure we seem to be about where our individual experience begins and ends. Each individual may choose a role (making it feel like part of the self), but alternatively he may find himself in a role as a consequence of factors beyond his grasp (unconscious family dynamics, nonverbal interpersonal pressures, hidden ethnic or social identifications), making it feel somewhat alien. Tom's story begins to raise the central question of this book: What are the steps toward taking up the role of active citizen?

These are dilemmas for all of us. We are each embedded in many groups—many more than we realize. Their tasks and meanings are in our minds if we search for them. Facing conflict with another, we might be able to allow ourselves to wonder which groups might link the differing perspectives we are hearing and feeling. And we might consider negotiating this shared membership with others in order to discover a way out of disconnection and impasse.

There are limitations to this method of exploration. If I am in a dialogue with someone who threatens me physically, can I attempt to find a larger context that joins us without being naïve? Physical danger inevitably limits negotiation. Tom said "back off" to the adolescents at some personal risk. He set a limit and contained their aggression, a precondition for exploration and discovery.

* * *

I've offered three stories. The first, a simple social example, is about taking up a leadership role in order to claim a shared space for a divergent colleague; the second concerns an individual and a group discovering their shared institutional task; and the third is about a man finding himself compelled to take up the role of a responsible citizen. All three stories are about listening to how the other is right and discovering and joining a shared context.

Václav Havel once said, "Hope is not the conviction that something will turn out well, but the certainty that something makes sense regardless of how it turns out." In our chaotic world, where exclusive and disrespectful groups (both "ours" and "theirs") do violence to those they perceive as outsiders, the effort to set a limit to aggression, to listen to how the other is right in terms of shedding new meaning, and to search for a larger context that joins, makes sense, and creates the possibility of understanding. In a relatively secure and contained context, joining something larger offers both hope and the discovery of aspects of others that evoke respectful listening. These are the first steps toward finding a citizen voice.

CHAPTER TWO

Containment and Communication

Listening for how others might be right is the first step in joining an organization. But what do we do with our strong feelings, our irrationality? We live within dynamic human systems. The roles and tasks of these systems are access points for grasping and acknowledging shared pressures. When intense emotions make clear thinking difficult, some form of containment is necessary so that people can hold still long enough to place their reactions in perspective.

In the previous chapter, when facing the adolescents' aggression on the bus, Tom knew he had to contain it. He set limits to create space for recognizing and joining in the shared task of providing social safety. One aspect of development comes from the experience of rupture and repair. The momentary rupture of dependable connections during the firemen's strike and the containment and repair, however transient, that Tom facilitated in the bus contributed to the development of all participants by underlining a shared social membership.

We learn how to contain our angry feelings in the family. Pediatrician and psychoanalyst Donald Winnicott (1960, 1963) described "the holding environment," a term that derives from the maternal function of holding the infant both physically and emotionally, offering empathic responsiveness, comfort, and safety.

When a child is angry, the holding environment refers to a calming parental response that helps the child not hurt himself or anyone else. When parents can respond to a toddler's angry outbursts with non-anxious, firm limit-setting in an atmosphere of love and understanding, they help him recognize that when he is mad at them, their reactions to his anger do not confirm his sense that they are "bad." In the face of his rage, his loving parents are not transformed into angry or anxious people; their loving relationship survives the storm. His parents are real, differentiated, and autonomous—and he can learn from them.

In the family, the clarity with which feelings and needs are transmitted and understood provides the child with a sense of safety and protection. A crucial aspect of this family holding environment is that it is negotiated (Modell, 1976; E. R. Shapiro, 1982b). Although it may appear that the mother provides containment for the child, in fact there is mutuality in the arrangement. The loved child also has an affirming role within the parent–child unit; the holding is created collaboratively. The family is an organization that carries out a task on behalf of society. That task is development. Each family role represents an aspect of this task and all members have the opportunity to mature.

Family containment also helps delineate a boundary between the family and the outside world. Once we begin to pay attention to the boundary between a group that is working on a task and the world outside of the group, we can begin to think about a system in interaction. When there is a loss of the holding environment in families, either because of illness, absence, or emotional unavailability of the parents, the family's developmental task can be derailed. Irrational roles (e.g., the "bad" father, the "sick one") can emerge as a signal of trouble. Not infrequently, this lack of containment can open the boundary around the family, bringing in outside intervention.

The consequences of failed containment

Openness to learning, continued interest, and the capacity to be surprised are characteristics of any organization working well. When organizations get into trouble, it is often marked by relationships that are characterized by *pathological certainty*, that is, when members think they know fully and without question who the other is (E. R. Shapiro, 1982a). Human beings are infinitely complex; our complexity is inevitably hidden from others—and from ourselves. Believing with certainty that we know one another leads to the formation of fixed, stereotyped images and the development of irrational roles (e.g., "she was *never* an affectionate child") that are not connected to and may interfere with the family's task. *Pathological certainty* and *irrational role creation* are two signs of trouble in all task systems.

In my studies of families of disturbed adolescents, I have seen parents inaccurately perceive or be unresponsive to the child's developmental needs. This failure of the holding environment is the outcome not of one pathological relationship, but a *shared family regression*. This is mobilized by developmental vulnerabilities in family members; it contributes to failed containment of unbearable feelings and resultant pathological certainty. The family as a system is always attempting to work at the task of development. But vulnerabilities in parents or children deriving from trauma in earlier generations (for the parents) or the child's sensitivities may require that the family compensates for those vulnerabilities in ways that obstruct the task.

In order to raise a child, parents identify with their children via their own experience as children. Though this can offer a useful perspective it necessarily brings forth any trouble they might have had in that role. Parents can obscure the changing reality of the child by their unconscious need to perceive their children in ways that reflect their own past. They then respond to the child as the child they unconsciously *need* (or *fear*), rather than opening the space to discover the child they actually *have*. And children are likewise sensitive to their parents' anxiety. Their inborn effort to maximize good care-taking by protecting their parents from discomfort can lead them unconsciously to conform to their parents' image of them, with consequences for their self-understanding.

The following excerpt from the couple's therapy of parents of a hospitalized adolescent reveals characteristic elements of holding environment failure in early childhood and the consequent development of an irrational role as seen retrospectively by the parents.

Father: Mary was never an affectionate child. Never. From the time when she was a baby. And it always bothered me. You could never hold her on your lap. You could never kiss her. I used to kiss her every night. I used to go in and kiss her goodnight when she was a baby until she got to be maybe ten, twelve, something like that. Every night I'd go in faithfully, and every night she'd pull the covers over her head and I would have to fight with her to kiss her goodnight.

Mother: Now I think she's rejecting us because we put her in the hospital.

Father:	She's mad at us.
Mother:	She is really mad at us because we did that.
Therapist:	What kept you going back night after night if she put up such a fight?
Mother:	I was thinking that, too.
Father:	Many a night we talked about that, too. We thought, "The hell with it, you know, this is ridiculous. I'm making a fool of myself." And I said, "Well, she's only a baby." She was then, and I just happened to think that children need affection, and I figured, "If she doesn't want to give it to me, I will show her I love her, and how else do you do it?" That's one way, certainly. Be close physically with her. Many a night I figured "Well, the hell with it."
Mother:	We had a tough time there. Something would happen, and we wouldn't for two or three nights, but it would bother us. She couldn't care less if we went in, and you feel like—well, you love her after all—you do like to ... Then it got to the point where Daddy would go to bed first, and she would come in and kiss him good night.
Father:	Under protest.
Mother:	She did that—but this was, of course, because we forced it on her, I suppose.
Father:	Yah.

In this excerpt, the parents are associating to their feelings of being rejected by their "unappreciative" adolescent. Parental love is always, in part, supported by a child's capacity to respond. Preoccupied with other feelings, the child might not be responsive to the parents' anxious need to have her confirm their view of themselves as "loving parents." The child's focus on herself can leave parents feeling rejected or abandoned, evoking painful and sometimes unconscious memories of their own childhood. If their "goodness" is not responded to by the child, parents can react with anger or withdrawal.

Here, the parents' defensive delineation of their daughter is that she has *never been capable* of love. This view of her obscures the flexibility necessary for them to accurately perceive their child's changing feelings and needs. Their anxiety makes it impossible for them to offer a more empathic form of love and to convey to their daughter that she can be mad at them without threatening their relationship. Mary's irrational role as the "unaffectionate child" is a symptom of distress in the family organization.

The symptom bearer as messenger: communication across organizations

The symptomatic and communicative role carried by one family member on behalf of a system unable to contain unbearable feelings can, not infrequently, mobilize outside resources to help the family get back to work. Not infrequently, such messengers are called *patients*. The following case illustrates the discovery of a family message unconsciously delivered by a child to a treatment system that had to learn how to hear it. The story is one of cross-system learning, involving a family and an organization struggling to integrate different but overlapping tasks: for the family, the task is *development*, for the institution, it is *treatment* (E. R. Shapiro, 2012).

> An eight-year-old boy is admitted to a child inpatient unit because of "unmanageable aggression." The psychiatric resident, overwhelmed by too many admissions, out-of-control and abusive patients, and disrupted families, carries out the additional paperwork for admission. The boy is one of five children from different fathers to a single mother. The boy's own father is currently in jail. The mother, overwhelmed by child-rearing tasks, is unavailable to come to the hospital after admission. The admission note indicates that the boy's aggressive outbursts are unmanageable at home. Recently, while the mother and children were shopping for groceries, the boy pulled a can of RAID off a shelf and began to spray his siblings. Terrified, the mother called the police, who brought the boy to the hospital.
>
> The resident finds the child lively, engaging, and not terribly disturbed. She is unclear as to why this child is in the hospital and feels irritated at the task of writing up a patient who does not seem to need her attention when she has so much else to manage. She presents the case to a supervision seminar with a focus on this community hospital's social responsibility to the local population. How can she get this child out of the hospital and mobilize social services to take care of him and the family? As is increasingly the case in pressured systems, a management response (mobilizing social services) is used as a form of containment to deal with the reactions of the clinician. She has too much to deal with and she needs to gather other resources to help her out; her pressures must be decreased. But were there any conceptual tools she might use to learn about her feelings so that she could contain and understand them better in the service of the task of treatment?

She brought the case to her seminar which had developed a group process with a focus on feelings as information. Although this approach challenged the prevailing institutional management culture, the seminar was able to hold the resident's feelings as the primary clinical data, inviting the group and the resident to perceive and use them instead of managing them. As the discussion unfolded, it became clear that all the trainees in the group felt overwhelmed by the clinical pressures; this was a shared aspect of the institutional culture. They could begin to recognize that these feelings were both expectable in this intense and busy clinical system—and essential information. They could see how these pressures were contributing to the resident's wish to get this child to another caregiver. Because the resident felt that a "good" doctor should want to take care of her patient and not get rid of him, she felt guilty about her irritation and could not fully acknowledge it. With the group's help, she could begin to see that her irritated feelings mirrored that of the harried mother who had too many children to manage alone.

This recognition generated a discussion about unacknowledged anger. When it is unbearable and uncontained, what happens to it? Where does it go? Does it get spread around the family and, if so, how? Was it possible that this child—the youngest member of the family—had empathized with the mother's distress? With great amusement, the group suddenly recognized that the child's attempt to spray his siblings with RAID could be understood as an effort—on his mother's behalf and on his own—to "get rid of these pests!" But, aside from providing a clever idea, how could this notion be useful for treatment?

The group began to recognize that patients who enter a treatment facility enter a dynamic system with its own unique frame and that the staff members who work within that system are necessarily influenced by it. In this particular system and in this community, too many needs and too few resources placed undue pressure on clinical staff and patients. In the face of these limitations, responsible caregivers might convince themselves that they should be able to do everything to compensate for the limitations. They may then, out of guilt and excessive responsibility, not allow themselves their full range of feelings including resentment and anger toward demands that are experienced as draining. When such feelings are unrecognized and not interpreted, they can interfere with work. However, recognizing and facing unacceptable impulses are the first steps in taking charge of them in the service of learning. Acknowledgement of painful feelings helps contain the impulse to act on them.

In this case, the supervision group helped the resident recognize that her irritation could be used to help her empathize with the overwhelmed mother. With this perspective, she could see that the child's behavior could be understood as a communication on behalf of the family system. This understanding allowed the resident to help the mother (who ultimately came in to talk with her) to gradually shift from horror at her child's behavior to recognizing that the behavior was an understandable communication about family stress.

The subsequent relaxed and supportive interpretation from the resident about the child's wish to "get rid of these pests" evoked surprised laughter from the mother who began experiencing the resident as an empathic ally. This perspective allowed her to tolerate her own anger, recognize that she was taking on more than she could manage, allow her to not be so frightened by her young son, and enable her to maximize her own resources and those of her children.

Active citizenship, in this case citizenship of the family, is by definition an interactive process. Spraying RAID is a form of interaction but in a language that in this case was difficult to translate. If the outside system can listen and translate such behavior into language, social development is possible. This child was functioning as a competent citizen of his family, voicing through communicative behavior his experience in a role in a failing family system to an external context that might be able to listen. If people are too marginalized to speak and their essential communications burst out through unmanaged behavior, society is deprived of the data necessary to help the community develop (Elmendorf & Parish, 2007). Organizational systems can be shaped to translate such social information.

Blaming the system

Psychiatric residents—like the employees of many contemporary organizations—are inevitably working in pressurized systems with too few resources. One of the ways they may manage these pressures is to hate the system they are in and blame it for the way they feel when they are working in it. This inclination to "blame the system" relieves them of their guilt about not having enough resources themselves (not enough education, perspective, clinical tools, or even empathy). It also begins to create an institution-in-the-mind as a garbage dump, a holding tank for all the unexamined negative experiences of the staff. Blaming the system protects us from recognizing that these are *human* systems; they are *us*. If we hate them, we remove ourselves from the opportunities we might have as members to transform them.

This happens in families whose containment functions fail, and it happens in organizations and in society, interfering with effective citizenship. If you hate your family, your organization or society, how do you manage your self-esteem when you continue to work within it? Blaming the system contributes to an increasing sense of hopelessness and can support a deadening use of management techniques or bureaucratic structures that systematically interfere with the possibility of engaging with and making sense of painful experiences in role—and discovering the potential liveliness of work.

Competently joining any organization as a member inevitably requires some level of identification with a mission and a set of values that link colleagues to something beyond themselves. In these pressured institutions, recognizing the realities of what the system is up against and joining the effort to work with an outside world that attempts to manage unbearable limitations supports the institutional holding environment and can be inspiring. Such commitment may require a reflective space to systematically receive, detoxify, and put in perspective the inevitable irritated and guilty reactions that such work evokes. With this perspective and containment, staff members—or citizens—can reduce their need to use the system irrationally as a failed provider and limit their projective use of other members (or other citizens) as receptacles for their own unmanaged needs.

CHAPTER THREE

Making Sense of Organizational Dynamics

In any organization, the pressures of authority relations, personality conflicts, and tension in people's outside lives can make organizational dynamics appear irrational and difficult to parse. How can we take seriously and make sense of the feelings that emerge at work—and how do we make use of those efforts to interpret our experience to clarify our engagement with the outside world?

Interpretation is a term that refers to a certain kind of information that provides connections, meanings, or a way of understanding previously disconnected data. Often, an interpretation is understood as the production of an individual: a person in an "interpreter" role gives an interpretation to another person. In my view, however, interpretation is better framed as a negotiation of understanding between and among people, not one that is handed down from one to another.

Any collective approach to the interpretation of organizational dynamics must take into account the recognition of uncertainty since every aspect of systems life is actively changing. These phenomena can, however, to some extent be grasped in relation to certain agreed upon referents. The basic referent for individual interpretation is individual experience. If I experience something, I believe that I know it for myself, given my life experience and my knowledge of my body and mind. So, if we have individual experience as a basic referent, how do we get to any shared referent that links people in agreed upon and deepening interpretations of interactive human behavior?

One familiar, if problematic, source of agreement between people about interpretation involves what I might call "attribution." Two people can often agree upon an interpretation of a third. The unacknowledged process of this agreement is usually something like, "Given that you and I are alike, and we are really different from him, let's interpret us as 'good' and him as 'bad' …" The jargon for this kind of interpretation is "splitting" or "shared projection." In social and organizational life, it is a frequent expression of irrationality, often occurring in relation to people in authority or to ethnic, racial, or gender subgroups. Examples of such interpretations (which inevitably include the subtext "unlike us") include: "the boss is on an ego trip," "immigrants are dangerous," "women are irrational," "men are insensitive." Such certainty may calm the anxieties of the interpreters who then feel that by arbitrarily defining someone or some group, they have mastered an area of potentially disorganizing ambiguity. It is, however, ultimately a way to extrude problematic experience by locating it outside of the self.

Attribution, however, is a basic human mechanism for the management of anxiety which we would not want to ignore as we work to make sense of interactive dynamics in social and organizational life. Therefore, the next few questions might be: How can I find an interpretive stance that takes attribution into account? If others see me in a particular way, for instance, what does that do to me? How can I maintain my curiosity in the face of my own and others' attributions? How do I know where to stand in order to see the appropriate data for interpretation? And, if I can get to such a place, how do I negotiate any shared interpretation with others?

In groups and organizations, one basic referent for developing shared interpretation is the *task*. For instance, one opening position for negotiating a shared interpretation might be something like this, "Given that we agree that we are engaged in this task together, how can we understand this behavior in relation to it?" Such a shared framework provides a partial refuge from unrelenting ambiguity and uncertainty.

This is not a new idea; over a half century ago Wilfred Bion (1961) demonstrated how people in groups and organizations are deeply connected to each other by their conscious and unconscious commitment to the group's task. Bion was a British psychoanalyst who experimented with leaderless groups when he was in the army. He and Eric Miller (1976) defined the "primary task"—that which is necessary for the group's continuance—as that which is carried out on behalf of its larger context which may be as vast as society. For example, hospitals take up the task of caring for the ill so that society can have healthy members and the family has the primary task of facilitating development so that society can have mature members.

Bion used the group's task as the lens to study the group's behavior from the perspective of an outside observer. From that perspective, he could discern two kinds of group behavior: that which was focused on accomplishing the task and that which appeared to be unconsciously dedicated to some other focus. He suggested that irrational process often took over in groups in relation to authority. Bion opened the door to an elaboration of unconscious dynamics operating in all groups. He described three types of shared unconscious assumptions in groups that took the place of task-related work: *dependency* (the group behaved as if its primary aim was to be taken care of—usually by a leader), *fight–flight* (as if the group's aim was to fight with or flee from the task), and *pairing* (as if the group could bring two idealized people or ideas together to rescue the group from the difficult work at hand). Though these unconscious assumptions can pull the group away from its formal task—and from the connection between the task and the outside world that all organizations must have to survive—Bion observed that they may also be mobilized in the service of work. For example, healthcare institutions mobilize the dependency dynamic in the service of care, the army mobilizes fight–flight in its effort to protect the nation, and the royal family mobilizes pairing in the service of social idealization and hope. When linked to the functional tasks, these unconscious basic assumptions can make work lively and meaningful.

Roger Shapiro and John Zinner, in their work at NIMH (Scharff, 1989; R. L. Shapiro & Zinner, 1976) added to Bion's ideas by recognizing that the unconscious assumptions they were seeing in families were more complex than the three that Bion initially described. Focusing on the family's developmental task and clarifying the related family roles allowed the NIMH group to deepen their understanding of seemingly irrational, but unconsciously motivated behavior that emerged in family interaction. This allowed them to begin to locate the struggles family members were having in their efforts to facilitate development. Their observations opened a more nuanced view of the range of shared unconscious assumptions discoverable in groups and organizations.

It is possible to recognize unconscious group behavior from an outside perspective. But what does any individual do to make sense of group dynamics when she is immersed in them? Here, too, the notion of task is central. Once we have joined a group and its task, we take up a role that is a function of that task and begin to have experiences that are shaped by that role. Though roles have formal requirements, different people take them up in different ways; some of those differences are shaped by our original family roles.

Family role and organizational role

The continuity from family roles to organizational roles is not always easy to discern. At the same time, people have an uncanny way of recreating their family roles in their organizations. If you look closely at the two experiences, you can discover otherwise hidden connections. Once discovered, such connections can be mobilized toward more effective engagement at work (D. Singer & E. R. Shapiro, 1988).

For example, in a study group that I worked with focusing on problems at work, participants were asked to provide as background their family histories. Each group member presented a current organizational dilemma followed by a summary of their experience in their family of origin. One participant focused on the complexities of simultaneously belonging to a number of institutions. The various bits of work she was developing within each institution could not seem to find a coherent home in any of them although they did fit together in her own mind. She inevitably felt that there were aspects of the work in which she was interested that seemed irrelevant to each organization. Within her main workplace, a mental health center, the small program she managed, which carried many of her ideas, could not effectively grow and develop. There were too many competing approaches to similar problems in the institution and no clear decision from the leadership about how to integrate them. Other ideas she was committed to had to be worked out within the separate institutions she was involved in; she could not find a way to bring the institutions or the ideas together. Her work dilemma related to the pressure she was feeling about finding a containing institution into which she could bring all of herself.

As she began to detail her family history, she described a childhood home with her parents living in her grandfather's house while her parents saved money for their own home. Her parents and siblings had limited space of their own; her grandfather brought in refugees to live in the basement (some of them very strange). Her siblings were much older, the place was filled with disconnected or curiously connected bits of relatives, friends, and strangers, tensions about who was in charge of what, questions about the containing structure and the appropriate boundaries of the family, and passionate arguments about almost everything.

She was the youngest child left largely alone to watch this chaos and develop her own interpretations of it. As the youngest, her role was to be a bit outside of the main struggles, not comprehending half of what was going on, invited to entertain but experienced as a bit of a nuisance. None of it ever made a lot of sense, though she spent a lot of time trying to figure it out. Why did her family have no home of their own and who were all these people?

As she put her early pieces of experience together in the light of her career presentation, much of it began to make sense. In college, she had majored in social sciences and had spent much of her time wandering through strange places trying to grasp strange customs. Even her dilemma of heading a tiny program in a chaotic, larger institution surrounded by competing "siblings" began to seem recognizable. The world could not be held responsible for creating such a similar role in her work life to that in her family life—she had done it.

The recognition of these parallels resulted in a significant lessening of the struggle she had been feeling. No longer did she find she was in a work trap from which she could not emerge. Rather, she began to see the ways in which she was using her family experience to understand something about the world. It was a perspective she had, a lens that was uniquely hers and that enabled her a way of connecting. She was trying to resolve a family dilemma and was using her workplaces to address it.

What became particularly clear to the group was the discovery that members were occupying a highly charged space in their organizations and work lives that closely paralleled key family roles of their childhood. They had somehow found ways of repeating such roles for themselves. Moreover, they began to realize that these earlier family dilemmas had for so long been externalized and embodied in their work context that they had difficulty knowing what was "in them" and what was in "in the organization." These themes and organizational dilemmas had become part of their life scripts.

In several presentations, we could see the power of parental authorization to "be" a particular way or engage in particular types of activity (e.g. assertive, nurturing, entrepreneurial). It had a significant impact on later occupational choices and ways of being in organizational roles. Negative authorization—the injunction to fail—was particularly striking and painful to recognize. As members made greater contact with these connections between life themes and work experiences, they came to realize how much energy was bound up in the struggle against their conflicted roles. With these discoveries came the release of energy; participants found themselves seriously saddened, angered, unburdened, and newly reflective.

Early family experience provides an initial emotional and cognitive map from which we all start in navigating our experiences in groups and organizations. One task of development is to enrich that map as we grow older, adding new role possibilities and alternatives. Our family roles provide areas of expertise, unique lenses, from which we begin to navigate organizational life. The places in which we get stuck in organizations are likely to be places where we are still dancing to old tunes without knowing it.

This perspective allows a connection between early family life and organizational role. The unconscious efforts to solve early family dilemmas can get lived out by the individual in the context of joining an organization. Recognizing and valuing the connection between family role and organizational role widens the possibility of more fully joining the roles in which we find ourselves.

Using organizational role and task

Organizational roles are the places where the individual and the organizational context meet. From that perspective, when individuals attend to their experience in role, it not only offers information about themselves—but also reflects aspects of the organization in relation to its task. These elements—task and roles—provide a relatively stable place from which negotiated interpretation can be made. In other words, my capacity to tune into my feelings and fantasies along with my recognition of my role and the task of the group allow me to begin to interpret my experience in relation to the institutional context. If the institution authorizes it, other members can do the same from within their roles (E. R. Shapiro & Carr, 1991).

What I am describing here is a way to perceive connections between internal and external reality in context. Of importance is the disciplined decision not to use fantasies and attributions as if they were a way of understanding other individuals, but rather as ways to begin to interpret irrationality in institutional life.

For example, a psychiatric clinic appointed a young woman to introduce a new program in child psychotherapy. About the same time, a new senior doctor was appointed. In public, he supported her approach, but she suspected that in truth he was ambivalent about it. Her anxieties began to focus around one small piece of repeated behavior in which the doctor would come into her office, furnished with only her desk and some small chairs for the children in treatment, and, while talking with her, he would sit on the desk and rest his feet on the chairs.

The trainee found this extremely annoying but, aware of her junior position, felt she could not discuss it with him. She therefore held the experience within herself and reported it to her psychoanalyst. The analyst suggested that she might be reexperiencing in this interaction with the doctor a familiar family role, namely, her early angry reaction to her father who she felt "stepped on the child" in her without loving it or respecting its value. Though this interpretation resonated with part of her experience, it did not connect with other parts, chiefly those aspects that involved her role in the clinic. She felt but could not articulate to herself or her analyst a vague sense that something important was being lost.

On reflection, we can begin to see what was happening: the behavior of another person (the senior doctor) was stirring aspects of the trainee's self with which she was coming to terms. Her use of this bit of data with her analyst was proper and reasonable in relation to their task of better understanding her early family experience and her life. However, since she and the doctor also had roles in the clinic where the shared task was clinical care, the interaction between them might also have represented an organizational dynamic concerning commitment to or ambivalence about a new treatment. Her irritation with the way the doctor apparently trod on the children (putting his feet on their chairs) might thus have been potentially as useful for the organization as for her private self.

The trainee's difficulty was that the more she attempted to grasp what was happening in terms of her own personal history and dynamics (or, for that matter, in terms of her fantasies about the personality of the doctor), the more problematic the experience became. In her familiar places—her transference world with her analyst and her professional world as a child psychotherapist (and no doubt in other roles, too)—she felt increasingly lost. She was unable to use her reactions to engage with and change her environment. She needed a way to gain perspective both on herself (with her psychoanalyst's help) and on herself-in-role within the clinic. It was not a question of one or the other; both facets belonged to her world and an interpretation that incorporated both was needed. In the absence of connecting interpretations, she was finding herself increasingly confused about the significance of her experience within a primary organization in her life—her place of work.

The notion of "role" is a key element. The trainee found that her assigned role provided the crucial link between herself (in her own treatment) and her context (in the clinic). Taking her experience in role seriously and beginning to make sense of it with the senior doctor in relation to the clinic's task would be a crucial step in her capacity to fully join the organization and its task.

The next step, however, to include the senior doctor in a negotiated interpretation, would require significant institutional support. For the trainee to confront her superior with his objectionable behavior, in most settings, would likely evoke a defensive and problematic response. If, however, the institutional culture supported collaborative interpretation and listening to one another for institutional rather than personal significance, the two staff members might be able to develop these ideas together (see Part II).

Task and *role*, then, are powerful tools for any organization to study itself as well as for the individual to begin to find herself in relation to the group. The orienting question, then, when facing organizational behavior that looks irrational is: "How am I (or we) working at the task?" Linking these role-related experiences within an institution helps define a shared context. When joined together, the elaboration of experience in role can illuminate otherwise unseen aspects of the organization. In this way, organizations can serve as containers of experience where individuals can link themselves to something larger yet still comprehensible. Studying experience in role, therefore, though often confusing, is more manageable than attempting to locate oneself as an isolated individual within the vast ambiguity of "society." The organization is an intermediate space between the individual and society where individuals can begin to locate themselves with others as a step toward finding themselves in the larger world.

CHAPTER FOUR

The Interpretive Stance

To begin to discern how an individual's experience can take on additional meaning in the context of institutions, Wesley Carr and I proposed a self-reflective model that we called an "interpretive stance" (E. R. Shapiro & Carr, 1991). It has two features of primary importance. First, the stance is speculative, imaginative, and heuristic. It allows the possibility of proceeding from one hypothesis to another rather than from uncertainty to certainty. At any given moment in any social or organizational setting, one or two of our roles are likely to be prominent in our minds. These concepts thus become the temporary structures in the mind within which and in relation to which interpretations of individual experience may be made. Such interpretation does not require special expertise or training—experience is always available and never devoid of context. Though profound emotional or organizational disturbances can shift us from this ideal, these shifts are generally temporary. Given the opportunity for reflection, even disturbing experiences provide vital data for an interpretation that can facilitate our discovery of connections to others. Using these connections, we can enhance our usefulness to our various organizational contexts, whether domestic, professional, or to society at large.

The second feature of our interpretive stance is that it allows people to connect hypotheses that originate in different sectors of their lives without producing confusion. So, people's experience as they examine it from the perspective of one role may lead them to a different place than when they consider it through the lens of another role. Since experience is indivisible within the individual the use of different roles as contexts for interpretation allows different aspects of experience to be creatively connected.

> An example may clarify these points. A company's stated policy is that it is an equal opportunity employer. Women and men, as far as anyone can tell, seem to be treated equally on the basis of proven competence. However, as a result of difficulties with her husband, a female staff member may be acutely aware of her gender experience—women are devalued or powerless; women are always put upon; women are treated nicely but not seriously. Because each of these expressions generalize in terms of "all women," this gender formulation may obscure the thrust of her own feelings: "I am devalued." We may locate her experiences in the context of the overlapping roles that she occupies—wife, mother, spouse, lover, but also business woman, executive, member of the company. Rather than trying (probably in vain) to disentangle these roles and claim that the experience of gender-related difficulty is particular to one facet of her life—probably problems at home—the interpretive stance would suggest the potential usefulness of reflecting on these experiences in the context of her role within the company.
>
> Examining her experience, from wherever it arises, through the filter of her organizational role, could offer clues about particular aspects of her work setting. For example, she may discover that in her organization women are mostly employed in underpaid support systems, such as administrative and housekeeping departments. Or she may note aspects of vacation scheduling that reveal an underlying, and hitherto unsuspected, organizational bias. The possibilities are endless.

If the organizational leadership authorized this kind of exploration and others within the organization participated in a similar reflection, her gender-related issues might not be so easily dismissed as her private agenda or as simply projected by her as a product of "the system." Within such a culture, she might be listened to in terms of "how is she right?" The interpretive stance assumes that individuals bring their own particular lenses for seeing the world around them. If a person is feeling acutely the dilemmas of gender issues, she may be more sensitive to and perceive more acutely gender-related issues throughout her interpersonal world that others may be overlooking. The clarity of her perspective, in conjunction with others' related views, might illuminate an aspect of her organization that had not been fully understood. This broadening of her experience does not diminish the realities of her home situation or her life in other roles. Instead, our interpretive stance takes seriously the indivisibility of individual experience: we cannot really separate our lives into a home part and a work part.

Those who adopt this stance possess and employ knowledge about themselves and their feelings to examine what is happening to them in a role. The stance is not one of specific cognitive expertise, acquired through study or through years of participation in a particular field. The people who take up this stance are best described as participant-observers in relation both to their own affective experience and to that reflected from people with whom they have dealings in various organizational roles. In using and interpreting their feelings in their roles, individuals stand both inside and outside themselves and both inside and outside their organizations. They become immersed in the dynamics of the organization and consciously try to discover within themselves and through their own experiences a sense of the issues that are important to the organization. They consider how their feelings generated in their roles reflect both organizational process and an outside perspective (Carr & E. R. Shapiro, 1989).

Individual experience, which has inevitable priority in all of us, thus progressively becomes a tool for engagement with others around a task. Three facets of this model link individuals' experiences to what is happening in their organizations and to the tasks from which they derive their roles: using internal experience, negotiating interpretations, and discerning the relevant context for interpretation.

Using internal experience

Internal experience provides the primary data for the interpretive stance. But such experience is not simply engendered from within. The practical skill the interpretive stance requires is differentiating those feelings that arise from without from those that derive from within. This is a complex task. We are caught up in and contribute to a profoundly interdependent world. Since we exist in dynamic interchange with ourselves and one another, to claim personal certainty is to deny an essential uncertainty about life. A fundamental aspect of the interpretive stance for each individual in any setting involves making this internal frame of reference, including what is unknown, usable.

Organizations may be thought of as collections of persons with experiences. These individuals may use these experiences empathically in the direct service of work, as is the case in organizations such as hospitals, churches, and welfare agencies. But people's experiences may also be indirectly related to work. For example, the introduction of modern technology has frequently generated in people powerful fantasies and feelings about their and others' dehumanization. Such feelings are often displaced and projected leading to alienation between sectors of an organization. Workers, for example, might attribute their feelings of dehumanization to the management rather than to the technology that occupies their work. Such collective defenses constitute significant aspects of the "internal life" of the organization.

By creating, managing, and developing a shared task, organizations and institutions can provide a holding environment similar to that first experienced in the family. But just as such holding is negotiated in the family, so does the creation of holding in organizations. Problems with negotiating such an organizational holding environment are often presented as issues involving communication and problematic relationships. However, though relationships are important, difficulties in negotiating a holding environment in organizations often have to do with issues of *relatedness*.

"Relationship" describes interaction between persons who are in actual contact in terms of the dynamic that is generated between them. "Relatedness" indicates that there is another perspective—no less personal in terms of the dynamic material—which examines the *structures* that such relationships create and their impact on and use by those involved.

Perhaps the example of the family will help to illuminate this concept. When I discussed irrational roles within the family, I noted how projections that occurred in relationships between members not only involved the individuals concerned but also affected the network that was "the family." Family members' behavior is affected by their relatedness to their idea of the family at least as much as by specific personal relationships. The notion of "the family," as it is collectively, emotionally, and largely unconsciously developed by family members, is a product of a shared projective process. It is in relation to this structure that shared unconscious assumptions about individuals evolve within the family context. Without a sense of this shared, unconscious structuring, it is difficult to address adequately problems in interpersonal relationships in any organization without getting locked into unproductive blaming and recriminations (see Chapter Eight).

> For example, in a large industrial firm with many subsidiary companies, the board of directors may never meet or see the management and workforce of a subsidiary. There is no personal relationship between them; this limits communication that might be used for reality testing since there is no actual encounter. "Those at the top," though never in direct contact, undoubtedly have an effect on the behavior and performance of the managers and workers of the subsidiary. This relatedness is not unidirectional: The existence of the subsidiary company also affects the behavior of the directors. Even on those occasions when there is a direct encounter, role relatedness has an impact through the way parties think about each other.

In a less emotionally intense context such as a company and its subsidiary, relationships may not be so discernible. The president and the janitor can scarcely be described as "in a relationship." But they each have ideas about the organization in which they participate and so each is connected to and through that to each other. As persons they may not be particularly important to each other but the roles that each occupies significantly affect each other's behavior even if they don't notice it. Thus, even where no discernible relationship exists, significant relatedness exists. All of this is to say that relatedness is one of the key frameworks for understanding individual experience in organizations.

Negotiating interpretations and discerning the relevant context

The fantasies and beliefs that individuals carry about the nature of their workplace has at least as much of an impact on organizational behavior as the workplace itself. To begin to make sense of an organizational context, therefore, means to examine the meaning assigned to any experience: Is it congruent with other people's feelings or is it idiosyncratic? If there is congruence, around what is it coalescing? If there is idiosyncrasy, why this particular type and why might it be located in this particular individual or role? In short, negotiated interpretation is concerned with the creation of shared hypotheses.

Whenever we consider shared interpretations, we also require an external reference or context that transcends individuals and their potential for irrational collusion. The frame of reference that meets this requirement is found in the organization's task. The term "task" here defines the reason for the organization's existence. It is, therefore, a concept that is immediately connected with personal feeling and organizational shape. I have already noted that the notion of organizational task is intimately linked to unconscious connections between people and the way these connections inform behavior.

We saw this in our study of the family whose task I suggested was to facilitate the development of its members. This would not, of course, be how any family would necessarily articulate it or even perceive it—even when they are deeply engaged in it. In some families the breakdown of an individual is a symptom of a breakdown in the family organization. Such a collapse is not simply the result of the sum of individual pathologies. It is a consequence or a symptom, and therefore an indicator, of the family as a unit or organization losing sight of the reason why it existed in the first place—namely, its task.

Every organization has a task or series of tasks around which people associate. These are not the same as the aims it endorses. These aims may be of an infinite variety—making money, being affirmed by success, filling employment positions. But people negotiate individually and collaboratively, through their organizational roles in relation to something that both transcends these aims and enables them to be pursued, namely the task, which links the organization to the larger society and thereby assures the organization's continued existence.

Although aims are not unimportant, a perception of task is crucial in maintaining a grip on reality. When the question of task arises, attention is immediately and necessarily directed to the connections (or absence of them) between an organization and its outside world. The idea of task, therefore, inevitably transcends aims—and personalities; in this sense, individuals do not have tasks since my use of task is a collaborative notion. It provides a referent that transcends the individual without diminishing his or her significance. It also transcends the organization and affirms it by drawing attention to its existence in the context of societal need.

Organizations and their members frequently and inevitably lose sight of the notion of task. But without recognition of its existence—even when all are unsure about its precise definition—interpretation is not possible. The understanding we seek emerges from the process of creating shared hypotheses about what is going on. Interpretation, therefore, is not asserted but is collaboratively created and thus has a major function both for interpreter and interpreted. The interpretive stance involves identifying individual experience in the context of a role and using such experience with that of others to create negotiated interpretations about the organization.

The interpretive stance affirms the significance of people's experience and feelings which may be chaotic and are often projected. But as in our study of the family in Chapter Two, they do not so much need interpretation from outside as a context within which they can be contained, affirmed, and utilized—a holding environment. This context—in both families and organizations—is shaped by the two fundamental notions, task and role. Individuals using this stance reflect on their experience within the framework of their roles. In so doing, both they as individuals and the organization and its task are affirmed. Organizations that adopt this approach develop as their basic mode of scrutiny a style of managed, coordinated self-reflection. The interpretive stance, then, involves grasping a shared system of meaning by coordinating the two primary frames of reference we possess: ourselves as individuals, with our experiences, and our institutions with their tasks and roles.

Using the interpretive stance

Within an organization, subgroups have differentiated tasks. Within each subgroup, members have particular roles that they occupy as individuals. These elements—tasks and roles—provide a place from which interpretation can be made. In other words, my knowledge of my body, my recognition of my role, and the task of the group I am in allow me to begin to interpret my experience in relation to the institutional context.

If, for example, I am a tall, white, deep-voiced man, I begin to know over time that the attributions I receive from others will be about aggressiveness, power, privilege, and arrogance. Some of these attributions will fit with my internal experience of myself, some will not. I will gradually learn that those aspects of my internal experience that have to do with feeling small, fearful, shy, and needing protection will not be picked up in these usual attributions. Therefore, while I will learn that these attributions about me are of limited use in understanding myself or in allowing others to fully know me, if I relax my defensiveness and take them seriously through the context of my role, these attributions may illuminate aspects of my organizational life.

If I am in a leadership role in an accounting department in an organization, I might begin to think about the organization's choosing me to be in that role and I might then ask myself about the organization's needs for aggressive presentation of accounting. I might then begin to connect this interpretation with my own attributions toward other people in particular roles and with my fantasies about other departments in order to begin to develop hypotheses about the institution's overall approach to its tasks. I might consider the possibility that my accounting department is managing some aspect of the organization's aggressiveness and begin to think about how the management allows some other aspect of the institution to work more freely with, say, passivity. Such an interpretive process represents a beginning individual contribution toward a shared interpretation. The next step is that of collaborative interpretation, negotiating these ideas with others and thereby moving beyond the mind of the individual into a collective understanding.

Underlying this perspective on interpretation is the notion that all institutions exist in the minds of individuals. In the mind, everyone works in a different institution, the image of which is shaped by the individual's needs, wishes, attributions, fantasies, and the organization's culture. Since institutions consist of humans and their irrationalities, the only comprehensive picture of the actual institution is one that is drawn from a collective and collaborative willingness to openly discuss the range of internal views and fantasies among the members. Obviously, such collaborative interpretation is unstable, shifting, and always open to question. Nonetheless, it does consider the dynamic nature of human organizations and their constant interaction and change in relation to their environments. The task framework provides a relatively stable container within which interpretive work can develop a dynamic picture of the ways the task is being engaged.

As I've noted, organizations take up different tasks on behalf of society. Attention to the differentiated tasks of organizations as well as the potential links among them offers an opportunity for individuals to locate themselves. So, for example, the army carries on behalf of the larger society concerns about protecting its boundaries. Since the army is doing that for me, I can be free of such concerns both as an individual and in my particular institutional role. I can then safely leave that function to the army, distance myself from it, and project my aggression into it, which irrationally protects me (and my institution) from an aspect of myself (and my role) that I may feel uncomfortable about.

Attention to the dynamic links *between* institutions can also provide useful information about social functioning. So, for example, in my role as a hospital psychiatrist, I can notice my irritation at insurance companies which limit the length of time my patients can stay in the hospital. My irritation clues me in to the fact that there is something about managing limited resources that hospital psychiatry has delegated out. The next question is, "Why?" and I then turn to the task of hospitalization for the answer.

Psychiatric hospitalization responds to patients' need for help in managing their chaotic and sometimes out of control feelings. Arbitrarily limiting the resources for hospitalization can mobilize unmanageable feelings of impotent anger (in our patients, their families and, not infrequently, in hospital staff). Seeing this, I can begin to question why the task of helping our patients manage angry feelings about limitations should be split off and directed toward insurance companies rather than held within the treatment setting so that these feelings can be acknowledged, borne, and put in perspective.

Acknowledging limitations and tolerating the aggressive response to them is an aspect of mental health. Recognizing this, I begin to think that this delegation to insurance companies is irrational and may not be in the service of my task of caring for patients. I then must think about how to incorporate limitations into my provision of hospital care (see Chapter Nine).

Using this perspective to look outward toward the larger society suggests to me that there may be a breakdown and fragmentation in society's efforts to help its citizens face and come to terms with limitations. This is an example of how the interpretive stance in an organizational role and developing cross-institutional thinking can open a lens onto society. Recognizing such a social problem then allows me to consider what I might do about it as a citizen (see Chapter Thirteen).

CHAPTER FIVE

Taking Up a Role: A Case Example

This chapter offers an extended illustration of the ideas presented so far. I will describe my taking up a temporary role, joining an institution's task, and containing and examining the experience generated in the role. I will outline how this set of reflections led to the beginning of a negotiated understanding of the organization and the relations of its internal structures to its changing mission (E. R. Shapiro & Carr, 1991). I have inserted text boxes to illuminate my reflections on my experience as I began to participate in this organization.

In the organization I will describe, the stated primary task was "to promote the study and development of the technique of group psychotherapy." The organization, which had been in existence for several decades, had developed a structure called an "Annual Institute." This event was a three-day gathering designed to represent the organization, to provide an educational forum, to advertise the organization and attract new members, and to respond to the affiliative needs of the membership. A major feature of this event was the presence of an "outside resource person," who was to give a series of workshops around a relevant research or technical theme. I was contacted and invited to be the outside person to present a workshop on adolescents and families.

In my invitation, I was asked to accept the title of "Institute Leader." The task was defined as the presentation over two days of a series of lectures around a theme. The specific meaning of the term *Institute Leader* was not clarified, except that my seminars would be the "leading issue" of the event. Indeed, my name and topic figured prominently on the promotional brochure with the diverse groups elaborated within. I was flattered by the offer and pleased by the opportunity to present my work; I did not pursue my curiosity about the title of "leader."

In addition to my lectures, faculty from the organization were to conduct structured and unstructured (so called) "para-therapeutic" groups, designed to study group process in relation to themes that reflected the faculty's own interests. The brochure suggested no relationship between my lectures and the group activities. In other words, the connection between what I was invited to contribute and the organization's task was obscure. Furthermore, it became clear that I was not invited to attend the final day of the Institute when various members of the faculty were to discuss my presentations on a panel. When I asked about extending my stay in order to participate in the discussion, I was told quite firmly that it was not necessary.

> This was puzzling. Why wouldn't they want me to join in a discussion about the material I was presenting?

On my arrival, I was met by one of the organizers of the Institute. I was introduced to some of the officers of the organization (not the president) but was neither briefed by nor introduced to the faculty members who were to be the group leaders. My role seemed to be that of guest lecturer; the meaning of the title "Institute Leader" remained obscure.

My lectures were well received and the membership (of about 300 persons) was responsive, participating actively in the discussion that immediately followed. My role as guest lecturer carried with it the experience of distance from the membership, with whom my only connection was a formal one from a stage. Encounters with members left me feeling somewhat idealized and kept at arm's length. The warm, open response I experienced during the lectures contrasted sharply with the tension I witnessed both between the members and their leaders and in those who were managing the various events. They invariably appeared hassled, overworked, and irritated. It is worth noting that this last observation represented my fantasy and denoted an internal comparison I was making at the time between myself and other "leaders."

> Since my title was "leader" and I was puzzled about it, I found myself identifying with the other leaders of the organization and comparing my experience with the way they were being treated. Why was I being idealized and kept at a distance while they were being devalued, overworked, and angry? What did it mean to be a "leader" in this organization and what was the meaning of my title as "leader"?

One aspect of my presentation was to be a demonstration interview with a family selected by a member of the organization. Shortly before the session, one member pointed out the president of the organization, referring to him (somewhat scornfully, I thought) as "crippled." He did, on close scrutiny, have a mildly deforming arthritis.

The family presented for the interview consisted of a mother and two teenage daughters. The parents were separated and, despite attempts to encourage the father to attend the consultation, he did not appear. The therapist who presented the family described the father's absence as evidence of his inadequacy. The interview focused on the theme of ambivalence toward the absent and possibly emotionally impaired father whose wounded pride had kept him from the interview. His separation from his wife and children had resulted in his being idealized, longed for, and covertly devalued. Part of the following discussion concerned issues of boundary formation in families and the complexities of providing an adequate framework for family therapy that would allow the therapeutic task to proceed. One member of the audience questioned whether an interview structure that excluded the father would make the task of family therapy (with its focus, in this case, on the parenting of the children) impossible.

In discussing the framework for family work, I became more aware of the problems in the framework within the Institute itself. I found myself internally and symbolically regressing in the service of discovering connections between my experience and the organizational context. I was beginning to join the organization.

> I discovered that I identified with the missing father to a degree, in that I, too, was a leader in name only. I began to think about my absence from the process groups that would be meeting between my presentations.

The family interview had been so moving, the audience so affected, and the issues so directly approached, that I anticipated that some reaction and response would be carried over into the intervening group sessions. I asked members of the program committee why there was no link between the lectures and the groups and suggested they might be missing a learning opportunity. Their response was that no one seemed to have thought of connecting the two. No one was in charge of managing the interface, which appeared to be an unexamined internal structure that impeded learning and, it seemed, interfered with my role as teacher. I began to feel more like the impaired and excluded father in the family interview who could not participate in the children's development.

> **This interpretive hypothesis was based on my feeling de-authorized as a "leader" and struggling with the idea that was just presented to me that the father of the family I interviewed was seen as "inadequate" in his parental role because of his absence. Were there ways in this organization that I, too, was "absent" in relation to the task?**

I realized that my pleasure about the invitation had interfered with my confronting the framework issues more directly at the beginning and that I had been participating, like the father, in my own exclusion. I was beginning to feel troubled by my experience in the role of lecturer, since I could not find the link to the primary task of learning.

On the evening of the first day, following some of my lectures, the family interview, and the beginning of the process groups, a cocktail party was held to honor the founders of the organization. I was surprised at the atmosphere of chaos and at the apparent disrespect shown by younger members toward the older generation, manifest in their continuing to drink and talk as the speeches were given. I found myself again thinking about the day's theme of ambivalence toward absent fathers.

The following morning, one of the founding members greeted me and offered me a paper he had written previously on the origins of the organization. The paper described the idea behind the Annual Institutes as an attempt to integrate didactic material and group experience. An outside "Institute Leader" was brought in and given authority to work with the group, both as a teacher and as an organizational consultant and reevaluator. The paper described how this Institute Leader was originally invited to meet with the group leaders prior to the Institute. They would then continue to meet throughout the three days so that the Institute Leader could facilitate the integration of the talks and the process groups, bringing participants and faculty together around a shared task of learning and consultation.

> This gave me a historical context that helped me to understand how dramatically the organization had changed. This kind of phenomenon is a frequent experience I've had in consulting to organizations. Something emerges in the unfolding process that deepens and clarifies a hypothesis I've been working on internally. Is it serendipity—or is it evidence that organizations as systems are working at a task and looking for ways, through unconsciously delegated "messengers," to communicate their trouble to someone who is listening?

The contrast between this description and my experience as a "lecturer" at the current Institute was striking. I felt a strong temporal and symbolic link between myself (as the invited but not included "leader") and the author of the paper (as a retired and now ignored founder). I developed a hypothesis that the emergence of the role of Institute Leader as I was experiencing it might represent the confluence of organizational dynamics. I speculated that the role symbolically reflected a dilemma and that this organization had problems of authorization, task and role definition, and boundary management that could be studied from the perspective of this Annual Institute. Specifically, it appeared to me that the Institute had defined a teaching role that was incorrectly titled and inadequately authorized. My role confusion, it seemed to me, required interpretation and this was leading me in the direction of examining the organization.

Using ideas described in earlier chapters of this book, I began to theorize that the process groups might each be presenting a piece of the total organizational dilemma as reflected in their relatedness to my role. But I had no data to test this hypothesis. As if by chance, as I was reflecting on this possibility, two members of separate groups approached me to discuss their group experiences.

One young woman recounted her experience of telling her group she would have to leave before their last meeting. The group had spent the entire session in a fury about her limited commitment. As a temporary member of the organization, I identified with her and thought of my own limited time commitment and my departure, scheduled one day before the end of the conference (a fact that was known to the membership). I wondered about the possibility that her group was working on that aspect of their relatedness to me, through displacement onto her. I pondered whether the issue of the leaders' limited commitment in this part-time organization might be important to understanding the system's difficulties.

> This is another example of looking for connections to my experience in role as presented by others. Having internally "joined" the organization, I could more readily identify with other members. On the assumption that the organization was working at identifying, making conscious, and solving an organizational dilemma, I considered the possibility that the organization's principals were recognizing that they had unwittingly limited what I potentially had to offer by not inviting me to stay—and were beginning to recognize that they were upset about my leaving early. In this subgroup, they were recognizing that they needed their members to stay through the entire event. Did this also reflect something about the limited involvement of their leadership?

Then a young man from a different group reported his group's dissatisfaction with their group leaders. Members talked of a formlessness in the group's work and speculated openly whether I had been involved at all in the group aspect of the Institute. Several members had asked their consultants if I could be asked to consult to the group. I considered the possibility that this dissatisfaction might reflect members' awareness (in displacement) of the severed links between poorly authorized leaders and the task of the organization.

Following each morning's lecture, I was invited to meet with half of the faculty (while the other half continued their group work). I was given neither task nor agenda for these meetings and the faculty members present had no agenda either. The time was spent discussing my formal presentation.

At the end of my lecture series, I met with the other half of the faculty, including the president and several members of the older generation. In my lectures, I had discussed Bion's group theories (1961) and mentioned my experience as an organizational consultant. One of the older members asked me if I had any observations to share about the organization itself. I replied that I had a number of thoughts about it in relationship to my particular role as Institute Leader, but that since I had not been invited to study the institution, I was lacking collaborative data. The president responded that he would be quite interested in my observations and the rest of the group agreed.

As I reviewed my experience with them, the faculty and group leaders joined me in actively exploring the authority dilemmas I had uncovered. Data were immediately forthcoming from the officers, the members, and the older generation in support of the following themes:

1. There had been a gradual loss of focus on the primary task of the organization. The economic and social pressures of sustaining private practices in a state in which practitioners lived at great distances from one another had left members feeling socially as well as professionally alone. There was some discussion about a possible shift in the primary task of the organization from an intellectual task to a social task, an idea that was supported by the presence of process groups at the Annual Institute without clear content and by the procedure of cocktails and conversations over formal speeches. Loss of links between cognitive and affective work within the organization paralleled the separation between my role and that of the groups. Faculty members felt disconnected, unguided, unclear about and unsupported in their group work, with no clear place to develop collaborative thinking and new ideas.
2. There was a sense of a loss of continuity with the past, with marked ambivalence toward the "founding fathers," who felt unneeded and patronized.
3. Deep splits existed within the organization. Leaders felt impaired, unauthorized, and limited in their roles. They spoke of feeling that they, like I, held only a token function that was contested by others and unsupported by the membership.
4. There were feelings of loss of direction, depression, and despair about the future of the organization that had not previously been voiced or examined.

The work of this discussion was intense and active. Faculty members found that my experience of my role clearly reflected their organizational experience and confirming data were readily presented. Although the Annual Institute had originally been designed to encourage open evaluation, anxiety about what might be uncovered had contributed to the defensive construction of barriers to prevent scrutiny. This was specifically manifest in the separation of the Institute Leader from the groups and their discussions. The increasing difficulties of sustaining private practice in the face of widespread competition had led to an unwitting shift in the task of the organization in the direction of forming ties of relationships and away from searching for integrated learning. Since this shift had occurred surreptitiously and unconsciously, and without negotiation, the leadership was impaired in all its work. This became most clear in the Annual Institute, where I had perceived it.

> This discussion began the work of what I have been calling "negotiated interpretation." To engage in this collaborative work—the beginnings of a consultation—I had to be invited to share my experience and the ways I was beginning to make sense of it. Without such an invitation, I would have kept my reflections to myself, since introducing them would inevitably have run the risk of being experienced as presumptuous and intrusive.

Shared, unconscious expressions of the impairment within the leadership were elaborated for me in symbolic form over the course of the weekend. These metaphorical guideposts included barring the "leader" from the wrap-up summary, offering the image of a "crippled" leader; expressing contempt for the founding fathers; presenting and intensely discussing a family with an absent father; longing for the leader's presence in the groups; failing to provide an opportunity to develop an in-depth relationship to the Institute Leader; and separating the affects of idealization (of the lecturer) and fury (in the groups). The data strongly suggested that these unfolding events, capped by the gift to me of the paper describing the origins of the organization, were unconscious group communications presented for interpretation.

Despite the demonstration of the need for a more formally structured organizational consultation, however, such a request was not forthcoming. The problems of leadership had been articulated and demonstrated, and the question about a shift in the primary task raised, but the anxiety about outside scrutiny had not been addressed. The ongoing division in the organization between the need for integration of various aspects of the work and the need for internal good feelings persisted.

Discussion

This serendipitous consultation emerged from my reflection in a role. It led the organization to reevaluate itself and scrutinize its connections to its environment. The case demonstrates how the interpretive stance both uses and requires serious attention to internal fantasies and associations and their testing against a hypothesis involving the organization's task. It makes use of the internal workings of the consultant's personality as well as projections from the group concerning his role. From this perspective, the distinction between the person in the role and the role itself can be considered. The use of internal experience, reality testing, and the task as transcendent reference provides the possibility of interpretation.

The case also provides an example of the way in which interpretation, as I am describing it, does not necessarily require a formally negotiated relationship. If a person can locate himself effectively in a role, interpretation can occur. Negotiated interpretation, however, inevitably takes further work. There are times, however, when the interpretive stance adopted by a leader can effectively change not only individuals' functioning in their institutions but also the institution's capacity for self-reflection.

Part II

Leadership and the Self-reflective Institution

This section focuses on the role of leadership in helping to shape institutions as way stations into society. Society is too vast for any of us to grasp. We gain access to it through our organizations. To maximize their potential as entry points for individuals to find the role of citizen, organizational leaders must find a way to enhance their staff members' ability to listen to each other's experience in relation to the mission.

I will focus on the unconscious dynamics of organizational life and the role of leaders in making the organizational context usable as a social lens. Beginning with a review of the pressures on leaders from a rapidly changing society, I then describe the group relations conference as an effective model for learning about systems psychodynamics. In Chapters Eight to Eleven, I offer an extended example of the institution I led, where our collective efforts to utilize an interpretive stance shaped a self-reflective institution that helped its members begin to develop a citizenship voice.

CHAPTER SIX

The CEO: Grappling with Systems Pressures

Attention to systems dynamics requires an effort to make sense of feelings and fantasies, those generated from within the individual and those stimulated by engagement with the system and the larger context. Anyone who takes up a leadership role in an institution must learn to make sense of this range of reactions in relation to the task. First, a leader brings in his or her personality, family experience, and political values. Engaging the system in such a way as to maximize the competence of the staff draws on all of these. Leaders also face the constant pressures of a rapidly changing environment, the potential need for organizational transformation, the management of multiple boundaries, and the periodic seemingly irrational demands of staff.

In order to respond to feelings as information, leaders need to learn about irrationality and group dynamics and be able to contain and make organizational sense of these dynamics in relation to the larger context. Staff can no longer readily find job security or a sense of belonging and identity in evolving organizations. To deepen the staff's work commitments, leaders must discover the connections between the staff's ideals and values, a meaningful organizational mission, and the values and needs of the larger society. In an increasingly interdependent world, even private organizations are now discovering their responsibilities toward the larger community.

To effectively market themselves and energize their staff, it has become clear that organizations must join this wider system of meaning.

Becoming a part of any organized group means beginning to participate in complex, dynamic connections to larger forces that are beyond our awareness. For example, larger group entities—companies, a church, a nation—have influences on us as individuals because of their connections to the larger society. And these influences encompass national, racial, or ethnic trauma, ideals, values, or past glories which can be mobilized at times of national emergency or during periods of personal anxiety, exercising a powerful influence (Volkan, 1998, 2006a, 2006b). Though we may not notice it, each of our identities is inevitably an "identity in context" (Erikson, 1950, 1958, 1968). Initially, we identify with our family, and then with other groups and organizations that are linked to particular social needs, values, and beliefs ("I am a psychiatrist", "I am a Christian", "I am from Google"). Such identification serves to ground us within the chronic uncertainties and ambiguities of social interaction while also influencing the manner in which we interact with what is unknown. But, that grounding requires attention to the organization's task and the ways in which engagement in that task shapes the roles and experiences of staff and leaders.

In a world of little stability, the role of the CEO is under enormous pressure. Market turbulence, new technologies, demographic shifts, and globalization have transformed organizational life. In contemporary organizations, the CEO must discern the shape of the institution, articulate and link the inputs of the various stakeholders, and forge a clear mission that relates the institution to the larger society. Managing the external boundary, the leader must elaborate the institution's place in a world of competition and help shape the view others have of it and its function.

From organizational theory (Bass, 1990; H. A. Simon, 1997) to studies of personality (Kernberg, 1998; Pelton et al., 1990; Zaleznick, 1989), behavioral observation (Hendry & Johnson, 1993; Kelly, 1993), analysis of group dynamics (Bennis, 1989; Hirschhorn 1988, 1990; Hirschhorn & Gilmore, 1993; E. B. Klein et al., 1998; Vaill, 1989), and studies of the impact of society on organizations (Heifetz, 1994; Kanter, 1989; Lawrence, 1998; Schwartz, 1990; E. R. Shapiro & Carr, 1991; Stacey, 1992, 1996), writers have dissected every aspect of the person in charge. There is a new understanding emerging of the connections between the leader's personality, the impact of leading rapidly changing organizations, and the importance of discovering a link to society. Institutions have shifted from hierarchic bureaucracy to teams, closed to open systems, structured decision-making to creative management, and cognitive analysis to affective and intuitive reactivity. In combination with globalization and the increasing interdependence of social and organizational life, institutions require leaders to be articulate in a new way. They must find the connections between their own passion, the institution's function, the organizational culture, and a connecting set of social—not individual—values and ideals that both energize the staff and bring the passions of the larger society to the organization and its work.

The leader as a person

Many studies focus on the heroic qualities of entrepreneurial leaders who stimulate their staff to organize work around a dynamic vision. In an era that favored centralized hierarchy, authority was based on command and control and leadership was seen as a personal quality of strong, charismatic CEOs (Bass, 1990). In our contemporary world, authority relations are being renegotiated, with leadership seen more as a characteristic of the system (Heifetz & Laurie, 1997; Hirschhorn, 1988; E. B. Klein et al., 1998; Krantz, 1990, 1998). Competent leaders require a lack of self-delusion, the ability to make intuitive decisions accurately without models or conventional data, the capacity to simplify complex situations to facilitate clear-cut decision-making, and tolerance for ambiguity and decisiveness in indeterminate settings (Pelton et al., 1990). In general, leaders are divided into types: authoritarian (traditional), transactional (appealing to others' self-interest through rewards for desired behaviors), transformational (influencing others through stimulation and inspiration), and the facilitative, consultative, and supportive leadership of self-managing teams. Leaders are responsible for a series of boundaries: authority ("Who's in charge of what?"), allocation of resources ("Who does what?"), political ("What's in it for us?"), identity ("Who is— and isn't— 'us'?"), and external ("What is our significance in the world?") (Hirschhorn & Gilmore, 1993).

At all of these boundaries, staff reactions are filled with powerful feelings and fantasies, providing information about the organization and its work. Postmodern authority requires the person of the leader to be visible in the role, intimately available for collaboration and negotiation (Hirschhorn, 1990; Krantz, 1990; E. R. Shapiro, 2016). This contributes to a sense of community; its absence can lead to staff isolation and disconnection. Leaders who offer vision but are socially out of reach of the rank and file are more likely to be given mythical status and have magical powers attributed to them, making it harder for staff to find their own competence (Miller, 1998).

Most CEOs are no longer the person who sits in an office making decisions. Instead, they wander the organization, interacting briefly with staff, gathering data, resolving tensions and conflicts, developing ideas and strategies; the modern CEO is a data node through which all information flows (Heifetz & Laurie, 1997; Kelly, 1993). Leaders are profoundly affected by their followers and require a high degree of interpersonal integration and maturity. Since leaders represent the organization and its ideals, staff members look to them to find their own commitments in role. Heightened dependence on leaders, however, can be a defense against the painful uncertainty and risk involved in mobilizing individual competence. The CEO's discipline must be strong enough to avoid the temptation to gratify staff dependency by impulsive action. Since the exercise of power and the inevitable frustration of staff's unrealistic expectations can contribute to a hatred of leadership, effective leaders must be able to tolerate and contain the impact of negative projections and manage the pressures of staff outbursts.

Effective management is facilitated by a heightened appreciation of irrationality, dependency, unrealistic expectations, idealizations, competition, and envy in organizational life. This requires an ability to be in touch with a range of feelings generated by the role itself, and a capacity to make sense of such pressures in relation to the organization's task (Hirschhorn & Gilmore, 1993; E. R. Shapiro & Carr, 1991). An ability to be vulnerable to uncomfortable or frightening experiences without withdrawing from work relationships is essential (Kernberg, 1998; see Chapter Eight).

Inevitably, the dynamics of the CEO's family, family role, ethnic traditions, gender identity, and other internalized social structures provide a variety of resources for managing organizational stress and contribute to the leader's developing vision (Hirschhorn, 1990; Volkan et al., 1998). Increasingly, leaders must be transparent about their motivations and the effects of their own irrationality. In an open system, they can invite others to discern what they themselves cannot see (E. R. Shapiro, 2001c). Acknowledging their own limits, leaders allow answers to emerge from the larger system, negotiating links between their own values and those of the organization (Heifetz & Laurie, 1997). This kind of integrated leadership depends on the articulation, negotiation, and commitment to a set of values (Vaill, 1989). The embracing of publicly shared values—and the development of a mission that shapes these values and connects them to the needs of the larger society—brings the person of the leader and the context of leadership together.

Leadership of changing organizations

Organizations have shifted from command and control, hierarchically managed systems—arguably appropriate for stable external environments—to open systems of delegated authority, self-regulating team functioning, and differentiated decision-making (Bass, 1990; Stacey, 1992, 1996). In the postmodern world, turbulent change in the external environment is not manageable, but in collaboration with others, it can be anticipated and possibly understood. Given the new web of information and task subsystems, leaders cannot grasp the social field by themselves. They need subordinates who own the work. In fact, contemporary organizations are moving toward recognizing that differentiated knowledge is distributed throughout the system (Heifetz & Laurie, 1997). The new paradigm is distributed leadership, where work becomes a process of negotiation between leaders, each recognizing the competence of the other or being open about perceived incompetence (Miller, 1976, 1998; see Chapter Nine).

Internal organizational structure should increasingly correspond to the environmental demand on the organization (Bass, 1990). This is not easily accomplished. In contemporary organizations, competing structures often exist. For example, hierarchic bureaucracy exists to preserve and ensure efficient operations of the status quo. In contrast, learning groups of managers operating in spontaneous self-organizing networks function to undermine the status quo (Stacey, 1992, 1996). This contrast leads to constant tension between control and freedom. In response to all of this, organizations in changing environments might feature lateral communication and adaptability, based on learning and on less rigidly defined jobs (Bass, 1990). Firms that operate in turbulent fields are more likely to share the power of decision-making inside their organizations.

In their task and authority structures, organizations can confer identity, give meaning, be experienced by staff as surrogate families, and provide defenses against the potentially disorganizing anxiety of living in a rapidly changing society (Jaques, 1955; Menzies, 1960). But, increasingly, organizations do not provide such security. The shift from hierarchical to more flexibly structured systems eliminates the reassuring dependent fantasy that at least someone is in control. Since the more familiar organizations that managed dependency (the family, religion, healthcare, education, government) are in disorder, without predictable membership or responsibilities, work organizations are under pressure to provide a substitute. The most significant psychological and interpersonal pressures on leaders come from frustration of these dependency needs (Kernberg, 1998).

While increased delegation can lead to autonomy, freedom, and discretion, it also brings about uncertainty (Kanter, 1989). Periodic downsizing and the increasing recognition that job security is elusive undercuts previously stable social defenses, evoking conscious as well as unconscious anger in employees (Miller, 1998). In fact, while the CEO's mobilization of the staff's passion for work is necessary for organizational survival, the uncertainties of organizational life can undermine staff commitments. In addition, previously recognizable organizational boundaries have become blurred with outsourcing of tasks, mergers, and a loss of distinction between suppliers and consumers. The identity once developed through organizational membership has shifted, since it is no longer clear where any individual belongs and which leaders he or she should follow. This is also true in the larger society, as national boundaries erode in the face of the international marketplace and ethnic or fundamentalist identities emerge in their place (Barber, 1995; see Chapter Thirteen). Discovering a relatively contained boundary within which negotiated interpretation and discernible connections to the larger society can take place is increasingly difficult.

In response to this increased anxiety, anger, and uncertainty, organizations often try to create teamwork and positive feelings. Such efforts may be useful, but they don't necessarily substitute for the impact on the system of those in positions of authority (Krantz, 1998). Those companies that try hardest to eliminate or ignore negative or ambivalent feelings toward authority may instead paradoxically stimulate the most resentment, mistrust, and suspicion (Miller & Stein, 1993). The role of CEOs is to respond to their own anxieties and those of staff members, finding ways of addressing potentially unsolvable authority tensions through open dialogue rather than pretending such issues do not exist. The anxieties stirred deep within leaders may be the most sensitive scanning and early warning devices available. These reactions can only be used if the organization values the subjective, irrational dimension of experience, allowing it to emerge and be placed in a task-related perspective (Krantz, 1998; E. R. Shapiro & Carr, 1991). The leader's use of self-reflective humor, bringing his anxieties together with those of the staff at times of organizational vulnerability, can function both as containment and as a deepening of a sense of community.

For example, responding to staff anxiety about job security, one new CEO told his staff at a luncheon the following story.

> A new chief executive comes into an institution, and the departing leader gives him three envelopes labeled 1, 2, and 3. The outgoing CEO tells him to open one at each crisis. The first crisis comes, and he opens the first envelope and it says, "Blame your predecessor." The second crisis comes, and he opens the second envelope and it says, "Blame the environment." The third crisis comes, and he opens the third envelope and it says, "Make three envelopes!"

Organization and institution

There is an important distinction to be made between "organization" and "institution." *Organization* consists of the day-to-day workings of the system, the policies, procedures, and structures of the organization's work. *Institution* includes the larger context and the way the institution's task relates to the outer world, carrying out work on behalf of the larger society and projecting an image of itself. Thus, all institutions are "institutions in the mind." Negotiating a shared internal view of an institution—and managing the external view of it—helps provide a holding environment that allows some of the irrationalities that we all bring to work to be sorted out.

Both "organization" and "institution" have to be managed—but differently. The *organization* has daily work tasks, some quite concrete: the ordering of supplies, paying bills, managing services, and providing benefits. These must be accomplished as efficiently and effectively as possible. To manage the *institution* requires attempting to articulate a task, a mission, that effectively maintains the institution's survival, meets a recognizable need of the larger society, and allows the institution to be recognizable from outside. An institution's mission is not asserted, it is discovered (see Chapter Nine). Once this mission has been grasped, managing the institution requires an ongoing effort to articulate and assess the images evoked in the minds of others by the institution's work.

Organizational tasks can be experienced as deadening or lively. Engagement in a shared institutional mission that transcends individuals provides a framework and a shared set of values that contain and deepen the commitment of the staff so that they can learn about, bear, and put into perspective their stressful work. Leaders must continually reassess interdependent links between staff, clarifying the boundaries within which the enterprising individual is free to work, and articulating a meaningful mission to help people ground their experiences in collective meaning. In doing this, it is crucial for leaders to allow themselves to be shaped by their cultures. Vision and mission then become a way of connecting leaders and followers, reality and fantasy, and the present as it is and as it might be. The collaborative negotiation of values and mission encourages staff members to participate as full persons rather than as technicians (Selznick, 1957). When this is successful, they can begin to recognize their authority to see society as citizens through the lens of their institution's mission and represent that perspective in the outside world (see Chapter Twelve).

Not all institutional missions make the social connection. For example, Apple's 2017 mission statement is: "Apple designs Macs, the best personal computers in the world, along with OS X, iLife, iWork and professional software. Apple leads the digital music revolution with its iPods and iTunes online." This concrete formulation represents no social ideals or values, nor does it indicate what such a "digital revolution" leads to. It stands in contrast to Steve Job's original, and more visionary social mission for Apple: "To make a contribution to the world by making tools for the mind that advance humankind." Job's mission can readily be grasped and felt by employees, leading, for example, to the possibility of employees developing a public voice and ideas that are grounded in experience about the nature of human advancement.

For many institutions, the connections that might allow their products and society's needs and values to meet remain obscure. For example, Sam Walton's original vision for Wal-Mart ("Bring large stores to small towns") was simple and engaged staff by articulating a shared business venture, but the social values connection was not evident. After all, why should small towns have large stores? The same was true for Dell ("Computers sold over the phone" and "To be the best computer company in the world") and Amazon ("an online marketplace for everything"). These are missions, but to what end? While Wal-Mart, Dell, and Amazon are currently financially successful as *companies*, they do not seem to have discovered and negotiated (as *institutions*) their connections to society's needs and values. Inattention to this larger social connection can be perilous. For example, when Dow Chemical decided to sell napalm to the United States government during the Vietnam War, the decision made business sense, but the national anti-war sentiment and the horror evoked by the destruction of human life produced dire consequences for the organization.

CEOs are at the boundary of all of these interactions. The way in which they collect information, collaborate to make sense of it, and provide leadership gives meaning to ambiguity, fits incidents into some structure and significance, and recognizes possible strategic implications. All of this requires attention to individual and collective value systems. To grasp the relevant larger social sets of values and link them to the organization's mission requires the leader to attend to the series of relevant contexts from the individual to the job, department, corporation, industry, nation, world, and humanity (Pelton et al., 1990).

Individuals construct their view of themselves in interaction with each other (E. R. Shapiro & Carr, 1991; Stacey, 1996). In optimum circumstances, beginning with the family, organized society imposes on the individual through identification a scheme of social values and ideals that are deeply linked to personal motives. Many companies set up systems of organizational values, which attempt to reflect the personal values of their employees. This has the potential to build deepening connections between the individuals and the group, since individuals bring to their companies the values that they have developed in their other groups—families, schools, and social life. Because of the emotional power of those values, they can create profound connections and a common language between individuals and groups. If organizations do not incorporate values into their missions, individuals can lose sight of the larger meaning of their work and their passionate commitments decay.

So, a company might prioritize openness, diversity, ethical management, communication, empowerment, excellence, profitable growth, or any number of other attributes (Harvard Business Review, 1992). These are familiar individual values, but they neither differentiate one organization from another nor connect to any meaningful contemporary social focus, such as health, environment, or the integration of differences. In the past, private organizations had to consider only those consequences of decisions that affected the organization. It was the public and voluntary organizations with more manifest links to society's needs that had to develop comprehensive systems of community values linked to their missions. With globalization of markets and the developing internet technology that connects groups and nations in an interdependent world, an increasing number of private businesses are noticing their responsibilities toward the larger community (H. A. Simon, 1997).

Real conflicts exist, however, between profit and social responsibility. If carried too far, a values focus can divert an organization from its necessary attention to profit, so central to its survival. In an effort to energize their staff, some modern organizations have disconnected the two, finding themselves involved in superficial and even perverse attention to spiritual values that are unconnected to their missions. However, the ongoing attempt to contend with the tension between values and profit has led to new forms of organizational structures (B corporations) that now link the for-profit structure with a commitment to a mission. When carefully structured, a clear mission focus linked to social ideals can, through effective marketing, enhance profitability.

The modern CEO does not drive and control new strategic directions. He or she creates favorable conditions for and participates in complex learning and effective politics. Given the rapidity of change, the central leadership role in contemporary organizational life is leadership of the learning process (Miller, 1976, 1989, 1998; Miller & Rice, 1967; Miller & Stein, 1993). Contemporary society challenges leaders to think in terms of a large interconnected social system in which the organization is located. To do so, they must focus on the effects of group and social dynamics on learning. These are the essentials behind the development of an interpretive stance. Any vision must be specific, anchored in reality, linked to action, shared by all, located in a larger social context, and developed over time as the organization and its context shift (see Chapter Eleven).

A focus on society's needs is difficult for organizations to maintain in our contemporary world. The elaboration of an international marketplace has threatened national boundaries, creating challenges to newly negotiated standards and promoting global consumerism. As individuals have struggled to find themselves in this changing context, they have increasingly turned to brands as ways of negotiating their identities with each other and their subgroups (Jewson, 1997). But brands are not enough to convey meaning; individuals inside and outside the organization long to discover a larger significance. One of the central challenges of a more integrated multiracial, multiethnic world population is to discover a network of values and ideals that allow for the development of organizational missions that convey meaning (see Chapter Fifteen). But where can leaders, who are at the edge of this challenge, go to learn about this?

CHAPTER SEVEN

Learning about Systems Psychodynamics: The Group Relations Conference

Nothing is as you think. Things happen, people change, the system takes you, and you struggle to adapt and find your place. It is an amazing laboratory for understanding how one's personal interests and agendas intersect with the interests of the groups in which we have to participate.
—Executive director, New York City human services organization

So much fell into place about how I was handling things. I'm a much better leader now that I can see how these dynamics affect me, and how I affect them.
—CEO, urban hospital

I learned to position myself more "firmly" on issues that I believe in and that I want to defend. Since the conference, I've been more assertive, knowing that running greater risks is the only way to stand up for what I believe in. It was certainly one of the most unique experiences I've had.
—Principal, middle school

Society's pressures impact how each of us perceives the world. What learning opportunities can help us to navigate and make sense of our experiences? The group relations conference is an experiential laboratory where individuals can immerse themselves in systems dynamics and develop their capacity to have a public voice.

These conferences bring people from all walks of life to a residential setting in order to create a temporary institution for the sole purpose of studying its dynamics. Over the course of the past seventy years, the Tavistock Institute for Human Relations in London, the A. K. Rice Institute in the United States, and other organizations around the world have developed these residential conferences to provide participants with opportunities to experience the unfolding dynamics of groups and organizations and to study their roles within them, focusing on leadership, authority, and institutional life (Miller, 1976, 1989; Miller & Rice, 1967; Rice, 1966; E. R. Shapiro & Carr, 2012; Trist & Sofer, 1959).

Between fifty and a hundred participants from a range of organizations around the world come to a residential setting where they live and work together for five to fifteen days. They are placed into small and large experiential groups that run through the course of the conference. In the middle of the conference, having learned to work in experiential groups, members have the opportunity to choose their own groups based on themes that have emerged in their conference experience to that point (e.g. passion at work, ambivalence, creative solutions, women in authority). Members join these groups as the themes touch their interest and each group develops its own leadership structure. The groups interact with the staff group to create an organization. In order to begin to make sense of the temporary institution they are developing, review and application groups at the end of the conference begin to link conference experiences to members' outside work roles.

While subsequent conference directors have shaped structures to respond to changes in society, it is still organized around four basic components: holding and containment, specific group contexts, shared group dynamics, and a determined focus on the group, authority relations, and the developing institution. The four components are combined in a skeletal conference design and interact to create opportunities for members to join, engage in, and study institutional dynamics.

The conference often takes place on a university campus during vacation. As the participants arrive for the first assembly, staff members sit around a director in a row facing the members. The director introduces the staff and talks about the conference in general, inviting the administrator to give information about the house, meals, and other domestic matters. The members have been assigned to small groups, each with a staff consultant. Places for meeting at precise times are important as a statement of the staff's commitment to boundaries. For the duration of the conference, the staff will provide opportunities to learn by attempting to make sense of what they see happening in the conference as a whole and the groups in particular. The staff's group interventions will be based primarily on the experience evoked in them by the behavior of the developing groups, their collective sense of the conference task, and their working relationships with the director and other staff. The staff will speak only to the group as they develop a picture of it in their minds, not with individual members—unless they represent a group. Members are told that though there is a formal schedule of events, they are free to do as they wish within the limits of the law. This freedom allows them to take full responsibility for their actions while the staff provide opportunities for them to study these choices as part of the learning.

At the very heart of the conference is an effort to grasp the intersection between the personal and the organization, with a view toward studying the impact of organizational dynamics on effective management. The essence of this approach is about learning rather than teaching, about the unconscious mind in relation to the conscious, and about the group as the creature of the individual and the individual as the creature of the group. In essence, this spare conference structure provides a unique chance to experience the self in relation to others and in relation to a shared task. Beginning to see yourself as others see you is but one potential outcome.

There are three major psychoanalytic concepts that can help to understand the learning possibilities in these conferences. The basic notion is that of *unconscious functioning*: we are all moved about in life by much that is internal to us but beyond our awareness, both as individuals and in groups. Our unconscious functioning becomes evident through *transference* and *countertransference* and the use of *projective identification*. Transference refers to the ways our internalized images of others derived from our childhood experiences push us toward recreating familiar relationships in ways that can obscure the complexity of the people in our lives. Countertransference refers to our unconsciously derived reactions to being seen as someone we do not feel we are. Projective identification refers to the way we unconsciously attempt to coerce others through covert actions to become the people we need them to be for our own unconscious reasons (M. Klein, 1946; E. R. Shapiro & Carr, 1991; Zinner & R. L. Shapiro, 1972). This unconscious coercion occurs both between individuals and within and between groups. Through shared unconscious assumptions, groups can manifest this phenomenon by developing rigid, stereotyped views of individual members or of other groups that remain unchanged by additional information.

These phenomena are intrinsic to all relationships. In a conference focusing on how individuals and groups (note how inseparable these are) take up authority, how we relate to and use people become important data. We notice three levels of group learning. The first is the heightened recognition that individuals behave irrationally in the face of authority. If, for example, a staff consultant in his effort to focus on the group as a whole does not respond to an individual member, the member may react with disproportionate outrage, joined by others. What could be happening? For the dispassionate observer, this is extraordinary.

The next level is the ability to recognize group functioning and see the ways in which conscious efforts toward collaborative work can be hampered by irrational thinking on the part of group members. Participants often find the experience confusing, frustrating, and occasionally painful. Recognizing the ways individuals caught up in group dynamics can get lost in this way, however, offers new perspectives and potentially greater tolerance of workplace irrationality.

The third level of learning involves a shift toward new ways of thinking. The participant discovers that perceptions that seem initially unquestionable are always open to question (Palmer, 1979). This requires developing a capacity for both involvement and detachment (Havens, 1976; Sullivan, 1953). If someone is to learn to lead (or even competently to follow), then this capacity to reflect on one's own involvement is crucial.

The components of learning

Holding and containment

Though these conferences do not use the language of empathic containment that I discussed in Chapter Two, sufficient holding for members is implicit in the conference design, particularly in the clarity of its boundaries (time, space, territory, and role). One task of the staff is to be dependable so that members can feel secure and confident enough to cope with the anxiety, aggression, confusion, and new learning evoked by the lack of familiar guideposts. Wilfred Bion (1977) described containment as the process through which an entity (the mother, the family, or a social organization) holds anxiety-ridden aspects of experience within itself in order to detoxify them so that chaotic experience can be converted into independent thinking. Staff members accomplish this by providing an administration that attends to food, lodging, and other housekeeping, through rigorous and reliable adherence to time and space boundaries, by attempting to put the group process into words, and by unrelenting attention to the task and related roles (Parish, 2007). Members are informed that the staff's task focus is entirely on offering members opportunities to learn about authority and leadership in groups, resisting invitations to engage individual members in any other role or in relation to any other task.

When staff members attempt to make sense of the unfolding group process without focusing on individuals, members can feel ignored and treated badly. Their narcissism may feel injured and their irritation evoked. For example, in a small group, as members struggle to link their ideas, they may wonder what the staff consultant is thinking; one may ask him directly. Focusing on the group and attempting to determine the group's response, the consultant might not feel he has enough information to respond. Other members might react with irritation to this silence, focusing on their frustration with the consultant. At some point, the consultant might intervene by pointing to the group's dependency, saying something like: "In an effort to avoid facing your own uncertainty about noticing, sharing, and learning from your own experience, the group is acting as if, in my consultant role, I have all the answers." Such an effort to speak to the group as a whole will inevitably be experienced by individuals as stressful and ungenerous, since such a single-minded group focus from the consultant ignores social niceties and the responsiveness to individual needs that are part of everyday life.

However, by joining the conference, members have authorized the staff to work at this learning task in this particular way. Irritated, or even idealizing, responses to those they have placed in charge of this task can then be understood as an aspect of a group dynamic about authority. When group interventions focusing on this dynamic are offered, members can begin to recognize how the group as a whole is struggling to join the work. This perspective, linked to the individual's experience of attempting to join the group as a member, constitutes learning.

Specific group contexts

Throughout the conference, sets of assigned groups run their course and end; new ones take their place; friendships are made and dissolve. But at all times, participants are taking up roles and facing opportunities to engage learning from four perspectives:

The individual member

However deeply he or she becomes immersed in the life and dynamic of the conference, the member remains an individual and as such is responsible for his or her reactions to fellow members, staff, and other groups. In particular events, the individual will have the opportunity to receive and give delegated authority. This generates its own internal and group dynamic.

Specific events

Each event, such as large or small study groups (focusing on the process of joining), inter-group activities (studying relationships between groups), or application groups (focusing on applying the conference learning to members' outside roles) is a subsystem of the conference, with its own specific task which evokes characteristic dynamics.

The moment within the event

Whatever is happening in the here-and-now of the group process is an entry point for new learning.

The conference as a whole

Given the focus on what is happening in the moment, any member's role in the conference institution as a whole will be difficult to grasp. The staff with the director, however, will be constantly working on grasping the whole conference, regularly offering their developing views to the members. These perspectives present members with an opportunity to locate themselves (and their groups) in the total system.

Group dynamics

During the conference, the member is located somewhere on a spectrum between using others to being used by them. Within the framework of events, individuals have the opportunity to work at the task of the conference—to study authority and leadership—with little explicit help from the staff except for group interventions. Inevitably, individuals try to establish relationships with other members, but at the same time the group is being conceptualized and interpreted by the staff.

Each member is thus facing diverse tensions. On the one hand, individuals talk with other members but given the spare structure, they are inevitably unclear about what to talk about. So, they try to find out about each other and discern what kind of structure they are working in. Given that each group has a staff member present, group members will inevitably also be talking about and demonstrating their authority and leadership in relation to the task at hand—and in relation to the authority of the staff. At the same time, each member is trying to find connections to the staff member consulting the group while the consultant ignores the member as an individual and only addresses the group as a whole.

An individual member who remains psychologically separate will find the consultant's comments unfocused. Since the consultant is addressing the group and individuals have hired the consultants to help them learn, the pressure is on each member to give up aspects of his or her individuality (i.e. to regress) in order to identify and merge with the group, both to grasp the consultant's interventions and connect with other members. As each individual begins to listen to other members' perceptions as potentially linking to their own (i.e., how are they right?) the group begins to form as an entity, listening and responding with collaborative thinking and shared experience. This collective surrender to a learning task and the group's effort to work with the consultants generates an interpretable group dynamic, focusing on authority.

The individual member works with what is inside his or her mind in the context of what others are both saying to and seeing in him or her. This experience is intense. But it also takes place within a specific event: a small-study group, a large-study group, or an inter-group event. Over time, the group begins to share unconscious assumptions (Bion, 1961). Though, as the conference institution takes shape, these shared unconscious assumptions inevitably become more refined and complex, initially they are of the three basic types that Bion recognized:

1. *Dependency*, in which the group becomes passive and looks, usually to its staff consultant, for rescue from confusion.
2. *Pairing*, a variant of dependency, when the group turns to a couple (a member–consultant pair, or a heterosexual or homosexual pair), who are seen as an idealized hope for producing a solution for the group's problems.
3. *Fight–flight*, a quite different and more volatile assumption, in which the group acts as if fighting with the task (or the staff consultant as

representing the task of studying authority) or fleeing from the work are the only alternatives.

Beginning to recognize these and other shared assumptions—through the staff's and, ultimately, the members' interpretations—as a collective flight from work, can allow members to refocus their attention on the task and the unfolding institution. In addition, each separate event is experienced and worked with as an aspect of the wider conference. For example, there are up to twelve sessions of the small study group in the schedule. This set of sessions is a subsystem of the whole conference. It builds up its own dynamic culture. Held in the same place, with the same members and the same staff consultant, it becomes familiar. Indeed, amid the stresses of a conference it may even seem like "home base." Yet this system also exists in relation to the rest of the conference and both influences, and is influenced by, the unfolding unconscious behavior of the group within the series of meetings. And all this takes place within the setting of the conference as a whole, which generates an "institutional" dynamic.

Within this whole, the entire membership—in separate groups, one large group, and varying inter-group events—begins to shape its dynamic interaction with the staff they have authorized to lead the learning task. A temporary institution is being created for the purpose of studying itself.

A determined focus on the group and the developing institution

Ultimately this approach makes the group unequivocally the focus of attention and interpretation. This is not done, as with a therapy group, as a means to assist the individual to develop greater self-awareness and understanding. Instead, the method is designed to provide a way of understanding the unique temporary conference institution as it develops; it is an opportunity for individuals to grasp the impact of human systems and their engagement in them. The individual discovers how he or she is always part of a social construct. Indeed, for many during the conference there may be an experience of personal dissolution: Where does the group end and "I" begin? But the group is always part of a larger group—for example, the temporary conference institution as a whole. And then individuals begin to notice that they are locating the conference in an even larger context, such as nations, societies, or cultures.

By the end of a conference, members have had the experience of regressing into joining a group. They've experienced and discovered the existence of unconscious group dynamics and witnessed and experienced the irrational, group-influenced responses to designated leadership and authority. They will have discovered that their unique inner experience has direct relevance to understanding and participating fully in an organization. Through their own active efforts to create an organization, they will have seen or taken up forms of membership, leadership, and delegation and noticed the ways in which leadership can be authorized or undercut by group dynamics. They will have witnessed the ways particular persons behave in particular roles and experienced the way aspects of their own person are used projectively by others. They will also have recognized the significance of boundaries (time, territory, task, and roles) for organizing and shaping institutional life and begun to develop a picture of how the institution, as they are carrying that notion in their minds, shapes work. Finally, they will have had the opportunity to begin to apply these conference experiences to their outside organizational lives.

All conferences are to some degree reflections of the social context in which they take place. They are not, and cannot be, isolated from society or a culture. But a central dilemma, as the conference ends, is how staff and members can sustain and make use of the conference institution as they have shaped it in their minds. Such a self-consciously and collectively shaped institution-in-the-mind provides a model for grasping some of the ways we create our social institutions and provides opportunities to learn how we might use them as access points to begin to grasp the outside world (E. R. Shapiro & Carr, 1991, 2006). While there are other ways to learn to be an active citizen, the intense focus of these conferences is a unique opportunity to link inner experience to organizational life and discover the ways we each contribute to social irrationality.

CHAPTER EIGHT

From Group Relations to Leadership

Group relations conferences privilege the study of individual experience and the impact of dynamic systems on the capacity to speak and to lead (E. R. Shapiro & Carr, 2012). These conferences have many of the components of real-world organizations, though the organizations they create are temporary. They have a primary task, a leadership and authority structure, management functions, and a membership. The opportunities of these events include a focused study of the dynamics of a developing social system. Struggles around authority and leadership impact the learning both from inside and outside of the temporary conference institution.

One of the requirements of effective leadership is to sort out what belongs to the leader as a person and what is pushed into him by the system (see Chapter Six). In this chapter, I offer my own experience in leading group relations conferences to illustrate some of the learning opportunities these events provide. Conference work taught me about the systems psychodynamics of the leadership role itself and helped me to take up the leadership of a developing institution (see Chapters Nine, Ten, and Eleven). The conference experience illuminated some of the dilemmas of leadership that quickly become salient in conferences but exist in relation to any organization. As in Chapter Five, I have added text boxes to illustrate my reflections on these experiences.

My role in group relations conferences has, over the years, been at times that of participant, staff member, and periodically that of director. After a number of years directing smaller conferences, the A. K. Rice Institute (AKRI), which sponsors these events, invited me in 1990 to direct three consecutive national residential conferences. The contrast between my manageable first experience as director in 1984 and my chaotic second national conference in 1990 illuminates the range of institutional and political pressures a director must take on and the impact of organizational irrationality on the leadership function. My experience will illustrate some of the systems psychodynamics learning that, when incorporated in a leadership role, can impact the ability of an organization and its members to engage the larger society.

Directing conferences

In 1984, two days before the beginning of a week-long residential conference, the director resigned because of the sudden illness of his wife. I was the associate director and it therefore fell on me to take charge even though I had never directed a conference before. I was faced with a staff I had not hired, an administration I had not directed, a venue I had never seen, a design I did not create, opening presentations I had not written, a membership I did not know, and a role I had never experienced. I was incredibly anxious and uncertain—but the conference turned out to be manageable and members and staff learned.

This experience was strikingly different from the conference I directed in 1990. That was the second of a series of three national conferences that I was to direct. By the time it began, I had already directed many conferences, served on the national board, helped found the Boston Center for group relations, had written a book about group relations thinking with Wesley Carr (1991), and felt ready to have the first training group in a residential conference in America. I thought I knew what I was doing. The resultant conference was chaotic. Wesley as associate director resigned from his role in the middle of the conference, one member became emotionally overwhelmed, and the board of AKRI took an unprecedented decision to survey former conference members and staff about my work, ultimately deciding to fire me from my contract to direct a third conference without explaining why. It was wild—and I learned a great deal.

So, what happened in these two conferences? What were the differences between them, what were the systems impacts on my leadership function, and how did I apply the learning to leading a real-world organization?

In 1984, though I had begun to write about organizational dynamics, I had no formal role in the AKRI national organization (E. R. Shapiro, 1982b, 1985). There were few projections into me as a person; I was relatively unknown. At the first conference staff meeting where I was suddenly to take up the director role, I was overwhelmed, and the staff knew it. I was one of them—a staff member—elevated on the battlefield to a leadership position. Open about my anxiety, I made it clear how much I needed them, and they responded with amazing fortitude. The experience taught me about interdependence, leading from the task, listening to how the other is right, relying on the work capacities of others, and negotiating a leadership role. The stress proved manageable, the learning was widespread, and it all seemed to work well.

By 1990, I was very visible in the larger organization, which was more integrated and political. The founder of the organization, who had developed Tavistock conferences in America, had primarily mentored men to implement her vision. Her apparent gender bias contributed to an underlying organizational tension. I was the last man she supported. She had asked me to help her establish a center in Boston and invited me to direct its first conference. I accepted. And, since I was chairing a national scientific meeting as well as working publicly with prominent senior men and women, I was—like Icarus—flying high (Carr & E. R. Shapiro, 1989; E. R. Shapiro & Carr, 1987).

> The founder's decision to select me carried prestige and excitement while evoking competition, envy, and feelings of exclusion from female colleagues, along with projections into me of arrogance, entitlement, and narcissism (not all of which were misplaced!).

Institutional leaders are always positioned on the outer boundary of the organization, engaging and paying attention to the external world, its political dynamics, and the external forces that impact the institution's task (see Chapter Six). This is true in group relations conferences as well. One of the director's jobs, as in all organizations, is to facilitate the staff's joining a negotiated mission. The staff come from the outer world and politics matter. As I approached my second conference as the national director, I knew that the organization was under political pressure to eliminate the founder's "old boy network" used in staff selection and begin to develop more objective criteria to determine staff competence.

Gender was a foremost issue and I was experienced as representing white male authority. Conference administration focused on taking care of the staff and members (food, lodging, etc.) This management was seen as "women's work" and was treated as second class to the consultant role that focused on interpretation (Parish, 2007). In agreeing to take on the directorship, I was aware of these concerns and confident that I could navigate an appropriate course to address them.

> My confidence came from a combination of inexperience and grandiosity. Though I understood the issues conceptually, I had little understanding of the feelings that others were carrying, and how difficult it might be to figure out solutions in the absence of more careful listening and negotiation.

My first move in responding to the politics around staff selection was to invite Wesley Carr to take up the role of associate director and lead a training group, asking him to develop public criteria (in contrast to the more covert "old boy network" choices) to authorize trainees to be consultants in the conference. Objectively, this was sensible: Wesley was from England and outside of the AKRI political system and he had a great deal of experience running training groups in conferences. However, though I paired him up with a senior staff woman to run the training group, I was blind to the fact that he was seen as an "old boy," tightly connected to me, and that he had little perspective on the way women in this American organization were feeling.

Then I invited the president of the organization, an experienced senior consultant, to take up the role of associate administrator in order, I thought, to underline the value of the administrative role and make public the opportunity to learn from that role. Focusing on the relatedness between staff and members, I decided to focus the conference theme on "interdependency." I couldn't have been more naïve.

First, asking the president of the authorizing body to become the associate administrator put both him and me in complicated positions. As the director of the conference, I reported to the president and board. When the president accepted the role of conference administrator, reporting to me as director, he was in a role conflict and neither of us saw it. This blind spot was a consequence of neither of us paying sufficient attention to or negotiating the differential *relatedness* we had in our minds to the national board (see Chapter Four).

Choosing Wesley as associate director was complicated; because of our recently published book, we were a very public pair and open to envy. It was also a risk for me to take on an unprecedented training group in an American conference as director without having experienced one. Furthermore, I was in the midst of a painful divorce and had denied its emotional impact on my directorship.

All of this affected the conference dynamics. As a self-reflective organization, the director and staff always study their own dynamics in public in order to facilitate the members' learning about authority. In the early stage of this conference, however, a group of women staff members met by themselves to discuss the glass ceiling and the dilemmas of female leadership. They did not see their discussion as conference-related, though the director, associate director, and associate administrator were all men. They refused to bring their discussion into the staff work, undercutting the learning task and their authorization of me as director. It was as if their conference gathering and conversation related to an event that I was not directing. Was this early staff rebellion a dynamic of the gender split in the national organization finding its way into our conference? We could not find a way to address it.

> This staff behavior acted out an organizational dynamic, removing from the conference learning task a set of gender-related feelings and projections. In retrospect I think this staff behavior was evidence that the board and I had not adequately addressed the organizational politics prior to my choosing the staff.

Then, in the midst of the conference, Wesley felt that the staff were blurring the two of us and he abruptly resigned as associate director in order (in his own mind) to clarify my role as director while keeping his role as director of the training group. Since he announced his resignation to the staff without consulting me, I either had to fire him and appoint someone else as associate director or take his action as a consultation and open my work more clearly to the staff. I chose the latter. Both of these events—the defiantly covert meeting of the women staff and Wesley's abrupt resignation—challenged my authority and revealed my vulnerability around the theme of "interdependency" since, as director, I was dependent on my staff and on my associate director. This unsettled me and contributed to staff anxiety. Then, one member became emotionally overwhelmed, mobilizing—among others—the associate administrator and increasing his concern in his outside role as president of the organization about the potential impact of such an event on the sponsoring institution. And finally, the training staff decided to recommend all but two of the trainees to consult, labeling them in public as not having met the new criteria. This embarrassed them and had a negative impact on the system.

So, there was vulnerability all around this temporary institution: my own stemming from my outside life, the outside organizational and gender dynamics infiltrating the staff and pulling them away from their conference roles, an envied male leadership pair with a new conference design, role conflict in the associate administrator, embarrassed trainees, and a visibly distraught member. It was a lot for the staff to manage, but we did manage. The staff's public work on their reactions to these issues was visible for the members' learning. In the ending groups of the conference, where members could begin to unpack their conference experiences and relate them to their outside roles, there was much evidence of members recognizing their own role contributions to their frequently vulnerable and seemingly irrational outside organizations. Their learning about authority and leadership during organizational turmoil was profound. The overwhelmed member went home safely and the staff and the director, though deeply stressed, survived—sort of.

Following the conference, the president carried his conference anxiety back into his role on the board. After reviewing his experience, the board decided to carry out an unprecedented post-conference survey of those staff and members who were also members of the national organization about the "functioning of the director" of the conference. This was a stunning move. The board knew that the staff were collectively responsible for the conference and they had no criteria for evaluating the director beside the formal contract. They were aware of the propensity of groups to use personality variables as foci for projection leaving unbearable aspects of the group dynamic in individuals. In addition, their survey only called upon a sector of the conference (some members and some staff), and they were reaching across the ending boundary of this temporary institution, the clarity of which we understood as crucial to member learning. As a result,

I became the target of the board's unprecedented and publicly shaming national inquiry.

> The blurring of roles between the board president role and the associate administrator conference role had contributed to the president's importing some of the conference anxiety back into the board. As director of the conference, I was responsible for having selected him, but the board had responsibility as well. In the absence of a consultant, we could not think about it together and the complex organizational disturbance became loaded by the board's actions into me.

The members' responses to the board's survey were fragmented, most being focused on their experiences of small and large groups, with only distant and confused images of me in my leadership role. The board was left to contend with the images and experience of my public vulnerability and anxiety during the conference, significantly emphasized by the president through his experience as associate administrator. When the board then summoned me to a meeting in California to face an unprecedented inquiry, I asked for a consultant to be present to help keep the conversation rational. When my request was refused, I mailed a detailed conference report to the board (as my contract required) and to every center president, declined to come to the board meeting, and resigned as director of the next conference. The board refused to accept my resignation and, after a secret discussion, in a 4:3 vote, decided to fire me from my contract, with no reasons given. All of this evoked a prolonged period of organizational gossip marked by formal presentations and a book chapter attempting to make sense of this conference and the organization's response (Fraher, 2004; Lofgren, 1991, 1992). Many senior people in the organization, including the founder, resigned from the national organization in protest and the subsequent organizational disarray lasted for decades.

Directing the Austen Riggs Center

A year later, I took up the role as medical director/CEO of the Austen Riggs Center, a psychodynamic hospital and residential treatment center focusing on "treatment resistant psychiatric patients" (Plakun, 2011; E. R. Shapiro, 1997a, 1997b, 2009; E. R. Shapiro & Plakun, 2009). Being CEO was stressful but there was a straightforward application of what I learned from the earlier 1984 conference. As was the case then, I had never led a permanent institution, was faced with a staff I had not hired, an administration I had not directed, a venue I did not understand, an institutional design I did not create, and a patient population I did not know. I was coming into an institution where many of the patients had made serious suicide attempts prior to admission; the work was intensive, long-term, and psychodynamic. The treatment setting was completely open with no restrictions, seclusion, or restraints. Riggs staff managed their work within a therapeutic community organized by the patients where the focus was on the patients' authority.

Despite all of the stress, I loved the work; it was a role that allowed me to fully engage the staff, the patients, the board, and a broad range of external organizations around a primary task and organizational commitment that mattered a great deal to me. And on reflection, I don't believe that I would have dared to undertake this job without everything I had learned directing and staffing group relations conferences.

Thanks to my learning from 1984, I knew I could enter the institution with my ignorance up front. I needed staff, patients, and board to educate me. Recognizing the inevitable transferences to authority, I had to convince the staff that I was dependent on them to confront me with my blind spots. I noted that significant problems in institutions were caused by such blind spots in leaders. Unaddressed, these could be experienced by the staff as power operations. It was not easy for them to take the risk. But when I was able to listen and learn from them in public, making my dependency clear, we could begin to learn together. At the beginning, I had to be consulted on everything. I demonstrated my conference learning that leadership belonged to the system not just to the formal leaders by suggesting that we all might follow the person who could most clearly articulate the task.

But what did I use from the 1990 conference? In that conference, I learned to take seriously my own limitations and vulnerability as a leader. I saw how my personality and leadership style invited projection and I had endured the impact of those projections. I learned that my narcissism and grandiosity could shape an attack from the outside when I failed my colleagues. From my experience with Wesley Carr in that conference, I had experienced the risky dynamics of pairing and envy. From my experience with the president, I learned about the need to be careful and explicit around role assignment and its relation to the task, and I felt in my bones the complexity of institutional authorization. I had been personally shaken by the 1990 conference and the national board's hurtful dismissal. I had seen how a collective regression could damage a beloved organization. But I had also learned that institutional projection into a leader, though painful, was survivable. As the organization's founder, Margaret Rioch, had taught me: "If you hold to the task like the mast of a ship in the storm, you can ride out the emotional turmoil." That was my experience in the 1990 conference—and it helped shape my experience at Riggs.

Twenty years later, when I began to transition out of my CEO role at Austen Riggs, I could see the power of the generational issues, the hunger of the next generation to take up authority, and the difficulties in sustaining connections with those who had once been in charge. And strikingly, as I and the other four senior men were beginning to retire, the next generation of women that we had trained was in place to take up the leadership roles—just as in the 1990 conference.

My experience at Riggs taught me the value of articulating a mission that stood for a recognizable set of values and beliefs and linked the institution to the needs of the outside world (see Chapter Nine). With such a mission, staff, patients, and board could feel connected to something beyond themselves, allowing them to join in meaningful work across different roles. Our collective discovery of that mission—and our recognition of the need for an outside perspective when we lost our way—allowed us to survive the crises, tensions, and conflicts that accompanied the institution's growth and development (see Chapter Eleven).

Returning to group relations conferences

Shortly after I retired as medical director/CEO in 2011, the AKRI national board again appointed me for three years to direct their annual international residential conferences. Though I had remained a member of the national organization and worked on staff in a number of conferences in the US and abroad while I was at Riggs, I had not directed a conference since that fateful one in 1990. I had, however, become involved in several outside organizations that were applying systems thinking to social problems (E. R. Shapiro, 2001a, 2001b; 2012). The political polarization in America and the rising racial and religious tensions internationally led me to create related sub-themes of my three conferences, beginning with "What Do I Stand For" and ending with "Working Across Differences."

In 1990, the board had told me that I stood for privileged white male authority at a time of transition. That image affected how they ultimately treated me. Though I recognized and understood the projection, I had thought I represented something a bit more textured and task related. At Riggs, the patients, the staff, the board, and I found a way to negotiate more fully what I stood for as director. I brought that systems learning back to group relations work; it has led to the writing of this book. I had learned that the discovery of a place to stand and speak as a citizen can be enhanced by participating in an institution.

In the 2013 conference, my director's opening speech read as follows:

> "What do I stand for" is a question only an individual could ask. The question is a powerful one because it is linked to values, ideals, commitment, and passion. But once I as an individual ask this question, I begin to think, "How can I possibly know what I stand for? What if what I want to stand for and what I think I stand for is not the way others see me?" Even to raise the question of what I stand for requires me to consider the group. If I'm to live in a world with other people, my effort to discover the connection between what I want to stand for and what I actually stand for requires me to listen to and negotiate with the people who matter—in relation to the issues that are important to me. And those people are inevitably defined and shaped by a social context—a family, an institution, a political entity.

Amazingly, that 2013 conference, where a third of the members came from abroad, began in the first small group event with stories about the 1990 conference almost twenty-five years prior. It was an early challenge to my authority as director, and an illustration of how the past histories of leaders and their organizations can readily be brought to life in an institutional role. Focusing on what members referred to as my "failure and firing" in 1990, it looked like the reawakening of a chosen institutional trauma. The staff and I reworked the details of those events, beginning to grasp the underlying current conference-related question about whether the patriarchy (which I now symbolized in my role) had anything to offer to the next generation of women. The conference was asking if senior men and women were compelled to compete with each other for the hearts and minds of the next generation or whether the gender wars of the past could be sufficiently addressed so that the older generation of men and women might mentor younger people together. Given my past conference experiences and my irrational role in AKRI, I found this a deeply moving question.

In my opening comments to the staff at my third and last conference in 2015, I noted that authority is not just a feared boundary to be avoided, but also a longed-for boundary with inevitable vulnerability on both sides. The *mutual vulnerability of the authority boundary*, a deepening of the 1990 conference theme of interdependency, became a theme in this conference. The wish of the next generation to take up the reins, the wish of the elders to pass on what they have learned, the shared anxiety about death, the embarrassment of needing, the rage about dependency, and the envy and longing in both directions all factored into this vulnerability. Strikingly, the conference opened with an idealization of me as director, which appeared to replace the more familiar envy—and was more difficult to sort out, given its seductive power.

The staff's final message to the members in 2015 spoke to the vulnerability of authorization. Conference learning had illuminated how any authorization, any decision to take a stand, inevitably selectively calls on just those aspects of the self that are necessary for the particular task. Other highly valued aspects of the self (ethnic identifications, race, sexuality, vulnerability) may remain in the background, contributing to feelings of confusion, disloyalty, and impairment, bringing hesitation into the decision to speak. How much of the self can actually be brought to an authority boundary? Does taking a stand on behalf of others also signify loss—and can facing that loss strengthen authorization?

Anyone who approaches an authorized leader with needs brings vulnerability to the encounter. The leader's vulnerability and dependency are ordinarily not so obvious, though all leaders need their followers to help develop the institution. Mutual vulnerability at the boundary of authority, then, is a *fact*. It is ordinarily denied and managed through a series of defenses contributing to a leadership stance of pathological certainty and the assertion of a preferred perspective. That more familiar authoritarian stance can evoke anger, submission, or withdrawal on the part of followers, all of which limit engagement. Acknowledging vulnerability on both sides of an authority boundary, however, can be seductive, pulling for an idealization that also limits the possibility of engagement and learning. Though idealization can be a useful stage in development, the idealizing dynamic can unwittingly strip the idealizer of his positive capacities and hide the flaws of the one idealized. In this last conference, working through the idealizing defense was not easy—the staff dynamics led to significant concealment of sexuality, competition, and aggression. We recognized that acknowledgment of an authority's vulnerability is scary. It requires recognizing the need for the "other," and opens the possibility for love, hatred, envy, sexuality, fragility, and loss of role.

This focus raised many questions for reflection. Does vulnerability inevitably signify fragility? Can work deepen adequately in the face of this kind of affective availability on all sides? Is learning across differences and across generations so precious and fragile that risks need to be avoided? Would open aggression, competition, and envy incapacitate a staff that was open to vulnerability and potentially seducible through idealization? Would the presence of sexuality at a cross-generational authority boundary mobilize such unmanageable projections that groups would withdraw their authorizations, precluding the possibility of intimate learning?

In all my efforts to understand systems leadership, I still remain unclear about how much of the self can usefully be brought into the role, given the necessary projective use of the person. What is the impact of acknowledged vulnerability at different life stages? Is there a link between competence and vulnerability? All of these unanswered questions contributed to my further study of leadership and organizational dynamics.

CHAPTER NINE

Shaping a Mission: A Case Example

This chapter begins an extended application (Chapters Nine to Eleven) of the ideas I've developed so far. It is a brief overview of significant change and institutional learning occurring in a small psychiatric organization in the shifting context of healthcare in the United States (E. R. Shapiro, 2001b). During my twenty years as CEO of the Austen Riggs Center, a range of principles emerged that undergird the development of a self-reflective organization that can enhance the possibility for its members to find a place to stand in society. The core principles are listed below for easy reference and are illustrated throughout the chapter as I describe my tenure as CEO.

1. Discovering, developing, and shaping a mission requires initial attention to what is unique about the institution (its history, traditions, resources, skills) and an articulation of the social need that the institution can address.
2. Listening to the views of the mission from the various stakeholders (internal and external) and authorizing their perspectives can begin to develop a shared connection to the institution.
3. The system will communicate how it is working through its collective behavior, some of which might be directed at the leader, initially stimulating a defensive response. Beginning with an assumption that such

messages might contain crucial information ("how are they right?") can allow for the leader to contain his initial reaction, providing sufficient space to learn from the system and join it more fully.
4. Once the mission is shaped, delegation of authority and the creation of management structures that have clear connections to the mission can begin to develop distributed leadership and a collective ownership of the work.
5. If the CEO can work from an interpretive stance, acknowledging his blind spots, publicly attempting to make sense of his experience in role, and listening to how the other might be right, the staff can risk taking up an interpretive stance and begin to recognize that leadership does not entirely reside in the leader but in whoever can most clearly define the task.
6. Any institutional mission should have a clear connection to the outside society and its values and beliefs. These values should be clearly linked to this particular institution so that staff can readily connect their own values to their work (see Chapter Six).
7. When pressures from the outside world appear to threaten the mission, considering how these pressures might contain important information can allow the institution to sharpen its mission focus.
8. If the mission can be usefully condensed into a simple statement, each employee can easily speak about it and make it his and her own.

Entering Austen Riggs as CEO, I first focused on clarifying the institutional task as a link to a shared reality and to the larger society, authorizing the staff to take up the interpretive stance, and clarifying the range of internal management structures to support the mission. I found that it was important to underline for the staff the distinctions between power and authority. *Power*, I felt, had to do with the deployment of resources in such a way as to compel others to work. It is either task-related or not. In contrast, *authority* has to do with defining a task that people are willing to take up their own authority to join. The freedom to join (and represent) something that matters is a central aspect of citizenship.

These ideas initially derived from systems psychodynamics and the language of group relations work. As I entered Riggs, I found myself searching for these familiar landmarks in an unfamiliar culture. I subsequently grafted the organization's language onto this frame, developing a new language with the staff and the board through extensive, disorienting—and often painful—negotiation. With some difficulty, institutional mission substituted for primary task; personal boundaries (the "familiar" language of psychoanalysis) expanded to role, subsystem, and institutional boundaries; the study of large- and small-group process followed a public reassessment of the use of groups in the institution; and a shared recognition of institutional dynamics emerged from the gradual development of a culture of negotiated interpretation. I made every effort to be open about my experiences and to share my thoughts publicly as I began to make sense of my role, inviting others to join me in this endeavor as a way of attempting to understand systems dynamics through negotiated interpretation. The central dilemma in the institution was how to maintain the link to Riggs' valued tradition at the same time as it joined a changing world. To help the staff accomplish this, I had to introduce the unfamiliar while claiming the past. These linking concepts provided the necessary frame.

When I first arrived, the world of American mental health was in chaos as a consequence of the managed care revolution, a transformation of the insurance industry that focused on limiting the finances available for healthcare. As a long-term treatment institution, the Austen Riggs Center was significantly affected. At the time, the field of psychiatry was under major pressure from the larger society. Accusations of plagiarism, nepotism, misappropriation of funds, and sexual misconduct had forced department chairs of psychiatry to resign. Psychotherapists were causing scandals about the loss of professional roles with patients, court cases were emerging about the implantation of false memories of abuse, and long-term treatment was under close scrutiny. Fiscal pressures were changing the landscape, and psychoanalytic treatment was under siege from biology and behavioral science. The link between Riggs' mission and the needs of the larger society was becoming increasingly obscure.

Learning about the institution

Riggs was a distinguished, not-for-profit psychiatric institution whose staff had over the years made major contributions to psychoanalysis and ego psychology. It had represented the best in psychoanalytic theory and practice. Giants in the field, such as David Rapaport, Erik Erikson, Robert Knight, Margaret Brenman, and Roy Schafer had made significant contributions while at the Austen Riggs Center. Riggs was a reservoir of psychoanalytic thinking and one of the last psychiatric centers that provided intensive psychoanalytic psychotherapy for disturbed patients in a long-term hospital setting.

Prior to my arrival, Riggs had more than a million dollars in accounts receivable in the context of a six-million-dollar budget with a small endowment. As with many psychiatric institutions of the period, Riggs was organized as a hierarchy, with the medical director making all major decisions. There was no human resource function, and consequently no established institution-wide personnel policies or procedures. The administration of benefits often fell to the department manager's interpretation for specific individuals. Job descriptions listed a smattering of tasks but no measurements or expectations. Performance evaluations were missing. There was no differentiated compensation system, and everyone expected a salary adjustment every year no matter their performance. The place ran on oral tradition. When I asked why something was done, the usual answer was, "Because that's the way we've always done it." Managers were not trained in management. In response to newly developing external accrediting pressures, brilliant clinicians had taken up quasi-administrative roles which they experienced as "tacked-on responsibilities."

The institution was entirely focused on the needs of the patients; it did not have the infrastructure necessary for a changing environment. Administrators handled employee issues without grasping the impact on the wider system or considering the systems implications of staff dynamics on patient care. The staff barely discussed or attempted to understand what was going on in the larger system. Individual psychotherapy was the dominant discipline; there was one full-time social worker. Nursing staff felt devalued and therapists used them as supports for the psychotherapy.

The dynamics of the institution indicated a systematic confusion between power and authority. Authority derives from a shared task, and members of different subgroups in the institution were not in agreement about what that task was. My concern was that in a system that used power without a clear connection to a task, individuals can feel abused. This experience is often accompanied by splitting and projection, which I saw between the board and the staff. I had learned that a shared and agreed-upon task can serve as an abstract "third party" that allows members to bridge their polarized connections and grasp a shared reality. The question was how to define it. In the year prior to my taking up my new position, the board of trustees and the medical director invited me to take up the role of consultant to the board.

Renegotiating the mission (Principles 1 and 2)

I realized that not only did I not know what institution I was joining, the staff and the board did not know what medical director they were getting. With the authorization of the board, I set up a structure from Boston to renegotiate a mission. I invited patients, staff, and the board to organize subgroups within each role for the purpose of articulating their distinctive views of the center's mission. I asked each subgroup to authorize representatives to negotiate the differences. Finally, I asked the entire system to authorize representatives to negotiate a final version of the mission with me. The process revitalized us all. Each subgroup engaged in lively discussions that helped them to clarify their values and beliefs and their ownership of the institution and its traditions. Each group articulated distinctive but overlapping areas. The final negotiation allowed me more fully to grasp the institution and discover the connections I was bringing in from the outside.

Much of what I added linked the institution's values to the realities of the outer world. The final statement was complex, but clearly articulated both the center's traditions and some hopes I had about its links to the outside. The process also authorized me to take up the role of medical director/CEO. The negotiated mission became the context for our work over the first three years.

Symbolic communication from the staff (Principle 3)

Senior medical staff sat together at lunch. Shortly after I arrived, I joined them, taking the seat at the head of the table. As I sat, there was a sharp intake of breath and several said to me at once: "You can't sit there!" I got up. Staff members informed me that the seat was reserved for the most senior clinician in the institution (a former director of psychotherapy); it was his seat. Listening to how they were right allowed me to see that this confrontation was a sentinel event, symbolically alerting me that in order to take up my role I had to attend to the power of the tradition already in place. I took this very seriously. This clinician was one of three partially retired senior staff. They did not talk with each other and were never in the same room together. Staff members assumed a deep disconnection between them and found it painful. Not attending to institutional meaning, staff gossip attributed the disconnection to conflicting personalities. All three were held in awe by the clinical staff. As icons, they represented the center's great past. So, I invited the three for dinner. Staff members were shocked at my temerity but in fact, the three seniors were grateful for the invitation.

As we socialized over dinner, their institutional roles emerged. One represented the link between Riggs and Chestnut Lodge (another prestigious psychoanalytic institution), and the centrality of intensive individual psychotherapy. The second was the former director of psychotherapy, representing the therapeutic community and the open hospital. The third represented a connection to Erik Erikson and research at Riggs. I began to wonder about the institutional reasons for their disconnection. As I formulated this question, they began to tell stories about these roles, leading to a warm and engaged evening. I articulated the aspects of the institution I heard from them and invited them to represent these within the institution. They seemed delighted. Their agreement to work with me meant symbolically that the new administration had respectfully engaged the center's tradition. Over the first six years of my tenure each of these seniors became gradually more involved. The first began attending case conferences on a regular basis. The second became director of alumni projects, organizing former patients and staff in a developing association. The third became a research affiliate and joined the staff as Erikson Scholar. Four years after my arrival, Riggs hosted a gala celebration of the senior clinician's seventy-fifth birthday. I presented him with an engraved Riggs chair to place at the head of the senior staff lunch table, where he continued to sit until his death a decade later.

Shaping management structures (Principle 4)

Riggs had many brilliant clinicians and a creative clinical structure. It housed fifty patients in long-term hospital care, with a "step-down" program to less intensive care located in a separate building on campus. The hospital was completely open with no privilege system, no seclusion rooms, and no restrictions. Patients were free to come and go though many were significantly troubled. The center had a therapeutic community in which patients were invited to take charge of their lives and contribute to the functioning of the hospital. There was a unique activities program started by Erik Erikson's wife, Joan, where patients temporarily left the patient role and worked as students with craftspeople and artists. The intensive psychotherapy was well-organized and supervised, with a clear psychoanalytic focus and traditional boundaries.

The major problem was in the organizational structure, which was inflexible and outdated. Without a shared picture of the institution and its task, each department constituted its own world; the organizational atmosphere was filled with competition and rivalry. Information was a means of gaining power and control.

> One staff member said, "It felt like we were in the same boat, but each rowing in different directions."

As I came on board, staff immediately turned to me for decisions for which I had little or no information. They asked me to approve funding for various projects, but they had no data about comparative budgetary needs, priorities, or benefits to the institution. Delegation of authority and flattening out the hierarchy seemed essential if anything was to get done. I invited staff members to learn about the rest of the institution and take authority for decisions in their areas from housekeeping to clinical care. We began the process of negotiating what I needed from them and learning what they needed from me. This proved to be a slow process. Staff did not know me and weren't sure they wanted to take up any authority. Meanwhile, though staff took authority as individuals for the clinical work, their links to a shared authority and distributed leadership were difficult for me to discern. I had to be consulted on everything.

I broadened the executive committee and encouraged its members to notice my ignorance and interpret blind spots both in my understanding of the institution and in my style of working. I told the executive staff that I would speak to them about areas they might not notice and hoped they would work with me in a similar way. My invitation seemed unsettling. When several dared to confront me and I was able to learn publicly from their observations, staff members began to take up their own authority. They began to see that I believed that leadership belonged to the system (**Principle 5**). I articulated my view that the person who most clearly could discover and articulate the task in any particular situation became the leader. This was an unusual authorization and was felt deeply by staff members.

One noted, "Few executive gestures cost so little and have such immense impact as recognizing task leadership in employees."

It was difficult to grasp the way the clinical operation worked. The only role that seemed valued was that of individual psychotherapy. One full-time and one part-time social worker responded to social work needs for all the patients, and nurses ran a separate culture in the patient building. Aside from the administrator, a few business office personnel, and various credentialing committees, there was little formal administration. Dependency filtered down to the staff level with members complaining to me about issues but assuming no responsibility for addressing them directly. Staff would complain about a co-worker, but when I took disciplinary action, they would rally to the staff member's side in sympathy.

The result was a diffuse blurring of roles between nursing and therapists, and within each discipline. Homogenization of staff avoided feelings of competition and inequality and resulted in dilution of role authority. Staff could not be assigned responsibilities based on differentiated abilities and training, so delegation was limited. Staff in leadership roles tended to "do it all" themselves, both because delegation was not accepted practice, and because doing it all gave the illusion of being indispensable. This process contributed to stagnation in professional growth, fragmentation in operations, and a crippling of role authority. For example, department managers were not authorized to develop their own budgets. Instead the administrator would present each budget based on historical data, "with a little added for inflation." Consequently, managers felt neither in charge nor invested in finding ways of saving money. The problem was in managing a shift from dependency in a hierarchical power structure to interdependency and team functioning in a system with a shared mission.

To this end, I delegated to senior staff members unfamiliar directorial responsibilities: clinical care, education, the community program. I authorized the director of admissions to manage the external boundary around managed care and the changing healthcare world and asked him to take charge of program development. I hired human resources and marketing directors. I sent administrative staff to group relations conferences. As staff members took up these new roles, they began to negotiate with each other, feel the shape of the institution, and see the needs of the staff below them. Grasping a changing administrative structure was a developmental move for many. They gradually recognized that good administration was a way to provide for the next generation. They discovered the generativity in creating the conditions for good clinical work and managing an open boundary to society, all while becoming excited about the larger mission.

From my perspective, I needed colleagues to help manage a complex system. Once they joined, we could begin to discern the ways the institution was working together and examine the place that Riggs occupied in the larger society. Riggs' historical focus on individual psychotherapy and the professional power of medicine in a hierarchical organization had contributed to subduing the voices of other disciplines. Recognizing the importance of expanding an interpretive culture, we began an effort to strengthen these voices. Riggs had run on a model of large-group process for years. It had a morning conference, where all the clinicians and nurses came to review all the patients every day. People would say, "Morning conference decided this," and I would never know what they were talking about. The group seemed to organize itself through projections into the large group, where the voices of senior psychotherapists held all the power. Given that most patients had stayed at the center for two to five years, there was a shared sense of the collective, but I was stunned by the degree of irrationality that was contained (and promulgated) by the large-group process.

The large group seemed to me to interfere with the delegation of authority and responsibility, so I attempted to shift the work into smaller groups. Against much resistance, we gradually developed small interdisciplinary teams to oversee the treatments of assigned patients. This marked a significant change in the direction of interdependency. Staff worried that this new structure would eliminate the "sense of the whole" and interrupt the dependent connections held by the large group. To their surprise, however, staff found the change exciting. It was new to hear the voices of other disciplines discuss details of their work with patients. Patients began to be invited to team discussions so that they could join in thinking about their own treatment. Team leaders developed new administrative and leadership skills. The dynamics of the organization shifted from large- to small-group process: more coherent, differentiated, and graspable from the perspective of different roles.

Defining unique institutional values (Principle 6)

In 1993, in response to a shift in the accreditation agency, we re-articulated an aspect of the mission, focusing on the set of values that defined the institution (E. R. Shapiro, 2001c). This was an example of an external pressure that improved organizational functioning. Values are nodal points for staff and patient commitment and passion; articulating them allowed people more clearly to discover their connections to the mission. We underlined *the importance of human relationships, the dignity and responsibility of the individual,* and *respect for individual differences.* Our therapeutic community involves what Riggs calls "examined living," pointing to *the inevitable tension between individual choice and community need.* Patients at Riggs take up differentiated roles as patient, student, and citizen and we underlined *the importance of preserving those role distinctions* in our effort to support the patient's authority for the treatment. The community agreed that without any of these values the Austen Riggs Center would not be recognizable. Defining our mission and articulating these values helped to clarify our connection to society, making more evident the possibility for both staff and patients to have a public voice.

At the beginning of 1993, President Clinton gave a speech to Congress about his plans to transform the healthcare system by providing care for all citizens. Within thirty days the number of admissions in East Coast psychiatric hospitals dropped dramatically. Private practitioners, fearful of government intrusion, held onto their patients because they were afraid referrals would stop. With a dropping census, Riggs began to lose $100,000 a month. It became clear that attention to the internal world of the institution was not enough; we had to face our surrounding context.

We developed a small staff group that reassessed every job in the institution. We looked at what we absolutely needed to preserve the mission. The results led to a dramatic and painful downsizing, losing almost a third of the staff. This event was staggering for an institution where long-term staff had committed their lives and careers to a previously reliable culture. Though most of the departing staff members were able to find other positions, many remained in the small town of Stockbridge, where they passed their former colleagues daily on the street. The pain of this decision affected us all.

The process deepened our interdependency with each other and the patients. We placed more weight on the therapeutic community and on the patients' capacities to manage themselves. Expanding patient independence allowed us to learn more about the ways our patients resisted self-authorization because of unconscious delegations from their families and society that were meant to be held, locked away, and not interpreted. Patients taught us how they had become "good citizens" of their families and social groups, by identifying with unspoken directives about the roles they were to assume. Unconscious compliance with these delegations interfered with their capacity to discover their own authority. Our invitation for patients to become citizens in the Riggs community of examined living allowed many of these formerly unconscious family delegations to become visible (sometimes through their enactments with others). Beginning to recognize these irrational roles provided patients with perspective and the opportunity to feel more in charge of their participation (see Chapter Ten).

We believed that the managed-care perspective was shortsighted; mental illness is not a short-term problem and we felt that the pressure for short-term solutions would not last. We recommitted ourselves to our mission and to intensive, four-times-a-week, psychodynamic psychotherapy in a treatment community that offered the longest opportunity to learn from this work, but we decided that the survival of our mission required taking seriously what the world was saying to us (**Principle 7**). We began to include families in patient care and expanded the social work department. And since we were listening to how the healthcare world was right about there being limited resources for treatment, I organized a Resource Management Committee to bring together business people and clinicians to examine the management of limited resources and their clinical meaning.

This in turn prompted us to learn more about our own institution. As the Resource Management Committee began addressing the limited resources, they ran into irrational responses from patients, families, and staff. Denial of limitations, rage about deprivation, and projection of responsibility were common on all sides. The presence of clinical people in these discussions required negotiating a shared language. We discovered that "limited resources" was both a reality and a metaphor. The reality required management. The metaphor, applied to financial, emotional, and family resources, required discovery and interpretation for each case.

Staff and patients felt enraged about limitations but focused their rage on managed-care companies rather than integrating that feeling into the treatment. The Resource Management Committee pulled together these pieces and began to work with patients and families both to manage resources and to discover the appropriate metaphor within each treatment. These metaphors were much like a shared context. Connections initially denied through the operation of polarities could—through a linking metaphor—be named and owned. For example, an adopted male patient's struggle with limited financial resources could be linked to his unconscious sense that his father had died too soon, depriving him of the necessary resources to become a man. Interpreting this connection helped transform paranoid and unworkable anger into more manageable grief. This was an example of our interpretive stance, interpreting experience in role (both staff and patient roles) and relating it to a shared task (treatment).

This new language both energized the institution and transformed it. Staff began to help patients take charge of their limits and to understand the meaning of their reactions within their psychotherapy. The negotiation between business and clinical staff sensitized both groups to each other's world. With the patients' consultation, we developed a range of treatment settings at reduced cost which looked to managed care like six different programs: inpatient, residential, day treatment, aftercare, a halfway house, a residential apartment. Since Riggs was small enough for the same therapist and interdisciplinary team to follow the patient all the way through the spectrum, to those of us inside Riggs it felt like one program. Given this development, we renegotiated our external boundary so that we could both maintain our mission and allow patients, families, and managed-care companies to save money. The concept made patients' living situations more flexible and reduced ancillary staff. The new program definitions and boundaries were largely in the minds of patients and staff since two of these programs and the Community Center were in the same building. The collective work was to define a set of boundaries that would allow patients and families to assess—with our help—what length of treatment they needed, what behaviors they could manage, and what additional staff resources cost. With this information, they could select services so as to extend the length of their psychotherapy and manage the total cost of their treatment.

Joining the outside world and clarifying our mission (Principle 8)

We also helped the board of trustees to reshape itself in order to bring people onto the board with specific expertise in the outside world: marketing, development, business. We expanded our Community Outreach Program. The center's existence owed a great deal to the small town of Stockbridge that supported it. One of the patients said to us that Riggs was one of the best places she had ever been in because it was on Main Street in town, not tucked away from sight in the mountains. We felt we needed to give something back and link the institution more deeply to our outside society. Building on the Riggs tradition of helping develop the area's community mental-health system, we began consulting to local schools and not-for-profit organizations. We developed a Friends Organization of former patients, former staff, neighbors, and interested laypeople. This allowed us to develop a network of supporters and colleagues who could help us relate to the outside world, improve our marketing, and support the future of the institution. In other words, we began to articulate our public voice.

With the help of the board's marketing committee, we re-examined our mission statement and recognized that "the treatment and study of the individual in context" did not incorporate an outcome. We recognized that Riggs was taking a position in a larger healthcare debate between short-term biological and behavioral attention to symptom relief versus a more psychodynamic focus on helping patients to acknowledge, bear, and put in perspective the painful life experiences that had produced these symptoms. This formulation led to us defining ourselves as a national referral center for those patients whom the healthcare world called "treatment resistant," those for whom short-term symptom relief was not enough. We recognized that engaging these patients more fully evoked feelings of hope and defined our anticipated outcome as helping our patients find their own voice and claim a place in society (see Figure 1).

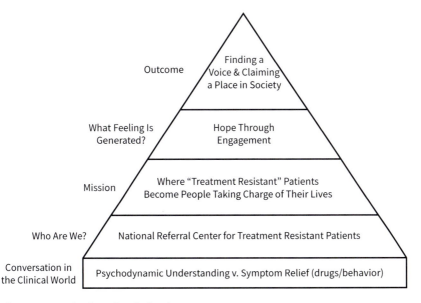

Figure 1. Developing Riggs' Identity.

With this perspective, our mission became: "The Austen Riggs Center: where 'treatment-resistant' patients become people taking charge of their lives." Taking charge of one's life requires attending to the larger context; it is a core capacity for a citizen ready to take a stand. We put the phrase "treatment-resistant" in quotes because our patients did not experience themselves that way; they experienced previous institutions as treatment resistant. And, one of our aims was to help people ultimately move out of the role of "patient." The statement concisely conveyed both staff and patients' commitments and passion for the work. It communicated clearly to the outside world who we were.

Managed-care companies defined their outliers as "treatment resistant", so we turned to them. Riggs was receiving patients whose treatment had failed after up to 100 short-term hospitalizations in other settings. We talked to companies about the fact that 10 percent of their patients—their "outliers" who did not benefit from short-term interventions—were spending up to 70 percent of their resources. We suggested that in the long run definitive treatment would save them money. In response, several companies developed contracts with us.

During 1994, the same year as the downsizing, Riggs had its seventy-fifth anniversary. With extraordinary work from a traumatized staff, we held an international symposium, hosting 300 people from eleven countries and twenty-eight states. Sixty former patients from five generations attended an unprecedented former patients' reunion. They presented a fascinating panel discussion on their treatment experiences at the center, one wearing a T-shirt saying, "I survived Riggs!" They reviewed the failures of staff in the 1960s to understand the nature of trauma. They discussed the painful implications of working with therapy staff who followed rigorous psychoanalytic technique without seeing the individual "in context," and recounted the difficulties they had experienced in the abrupt transition from full inpatient status to the outside world. These events stimulated press coverage and our census grew.

The treatment world was telling us that we had to demonstrate our results. We organized a sophisticated study of treatment outcome, focusing on the differences between symptom change (which is rapid and temporary) and character change (achievable only with substantial treatment). Promoting this outcome research was a difficult problem: It was expensive, very sophisticated, and uncertain as to its results. I expended a significant amount of "leadership equity" in convincing the trustees to support it. I felt strongly that we needed to do more than assert the value of our treatment; we had to commit ourselves to proving it. We had to determine whether deeper treatment leads to less resource utilization.

We were seeing that the effective treatment of our patients required close attention to their contexts: families, the therapeutic community, the larger society. In fact, the external context was embedded in both of our earlier mission statements. In 1994, Erik Erikson died, and we decided with the help of his family to develop the Erik H. Erikson Institute for Education and Research at Riggs. Having spent over a decade on the Riggs staff articulating the effect of context on individual development, Erikson was the perfect figure to symbolize our mission. The task of the Erikson Institute was to develop education and research at Riggs, bring in the voices and perspectives of other disciplines, and apply what we were learning clinically to larger social issues.

Focusing on citizenship

Toward the end of my tenure, we had begun to explore the following question: To what end are we treating our patients beside the more general outcome of "mental health"? The half-century development at Riggs of a therapeutic community program had laid the groundwork for patients taking up community roles. Freud had described the outcome of psychoanalysis as the ability to love and work. He did not mention "voting" (B. Simon, 1996). Joining a world of equals as a fully participating citizen is a central aspect of psychological health. Our newly focused mission lens—through which our staff could recognize congruent issues in the outside society—increased their capacity to offer their ideas as citizens. In addition, our therapeutic community of examined living that focused on the psychological components of competent social interaction increased the authority of patients and enhanced their recognition of and participation in the citizen role.

The constant search for the evolving organizational task that links staff and patients to each other and to the changing external environment served as a compass for grappling with these issues. It defined the identity of the institution, provided a matrix for collaborative learning, and served as a protection against the deadly narcissism that comes from institutional isolation and disconnection.

CHAPTER TEN

A Citizenship Laboratory

As I helped Riggs further develop a treatment system where the focus was on helping patients to be more in charge of their lives, I began to see more fully some of the psychodynamic issues affecting the role of citizen. To take up the citizen voice, as Tom did in Chapter One, requires individuals to discover their own authority rather than just submitting to another or turning the other into an enemy. Riggs' patients become members of a functioning community through what the institution calls "examined living," where their voices matter. Riggs' mission is about taking charge. How do members of a such a community interact? When their lives are so intensively studied by themselves and others, what do they learn? Are there aspects of the community learning in this institution that might help us understand what gets in the way of claiming a citizen voice in the larger society?

In this setting, we could see in great detail how problematic family roles get played out in relationships. For many of our patients, trouble in family life during childhood has contributed to angry feelings toward people in authority, which has led to withdrawal from social and political life, self-destructive behavior, or an unexamined interpretation of others as offensive. These are all recognizable elements of political process that contribute to polarization, where the experience and power of shared membership is lost and each side does not feel listened to. At Riggs, when the staff take up an interpretive stance and listen to how negative reactions might be accurate, such feelings can be contained and put in perspective. This enhances opportunities for individuals to join in a community organized around the Riggs values of *respect for individual differences* and *the effort to hold the tension between individual choice and community need*, both of which are central aspects of collaborative citizenship (see Chapter Thirteen).

The patients

Hospitalized patients with so-called "treatment resistant" psychiatric disorders have generally struggled to fit their needs within their human environments. Their early experience of a family environment that they felt did not respond to their needs contributes to these patients' lack of trust of people in authority. Treatment resistance may reflect this lack of trust. If the treatment institution itself can be structured to maximize interpersonal and systems learning, it is possible for patients to shift their negative relationship to authority (which in this case is their treatment), join the institution as members of the community, and begin to take charge of their lives.

Riggs' patients have experienced irrational roles in their families. They bring them into the treatment setting. Unpacking these roles and putting them in perspective means providing them with opportunities to see themselves as others see them. A contained environment that is focused on this kind of interpersonal learning provides an opportunity to decrease the use of others as "the enemy," an aspect of immature citizenship.

About two-thirds of the patients at Riggs have suffered significant early abuse, trauma, neglect, or other adverse experiences either in their families or with other authority figures. Their personalities have been radically shaped by these experiences. The disconnect between child and parents typically comes either from a constitutional failing in the child's ability to manage feelings or from an environmental one in which the parents' capacity to recognize their child's needs is interfered with by their unconscious efforts to relive their own childhood traumas through their care of their children. The combination can leave these children feeling unrecognized as individuals. A child's personality then becomes the way the child communicates the impact of these experiences.

Suppressing their anger, the patients at Riggs have denied the environmental failure and lived out their unconscious anger and despair in their lives.

They have withdrawn from engaging in a negotiation with the external world that might maximize their opportunities to develop. Instead, they unwittingly participate in consistently recreating the most painful aspects of their lives, one of which may be becoming resistant to treatment based on a fundamental distrust of those in positions of authority. Not infrequently, aspects of their personalities that they cannot fully discern may be difficult for others to bear.

We have learned that the best way to grasp our patients' struggles is to focus on the way they interact with people. All of us communicate our personalities by what we say and how we say it. Others usually notice more easily than we can how our process—the way we do things—transmits the essence of ourselves, including our most difficult aspects. In order to see ourselves in the best possible light, we either avoid or justify our negative qualities. To know ourselves fully—with all of our shortcomings—we need the help of others who both understand us and hold us accountable. And we need that self-knowledge to help us understand and put into perspective the powerful impact of early adverse experiences.

Clinicians are learning how our profession's current paradigm of treatment (focusing on behavioral and medical symptom management) has increasingly ignored the person, personality, and mind of the patient. Patients' ways of engaging the interpersonal world, their psychological structure, multigenerational history, and the subjective and personal meanings they have developed about their lives have become increasingly irrelevant to the field. While biological treatments can help patients reduce their symptoms, this form of relief—if not linked to psychological understanding—offers only a limited possibility that they will feel in charge of shaping their lives. The predominant biological paradigm for conceptualizing and treating psychiatric illness has led to the use of the label "treatment resistant" for those patients who require more than biological intervention—who need other people to help them take themselves seriously in order to change the trajectory of their lives.

In the absence of this listening focus, eruptions of uncontrolled behavior, disturbed relationships, suicidal despair, and an inability to contain intense impulses disrupt the lives and treatment of these patients. Periodic short-term hospitalizations for crisis management that focus on the imposition of external structure and behavioral and psychopharmacologic interventions are typical, but they are often unable to sustain these patients' stability after discharge.

For these patients, the repetitive behavioral struggle inherent in treatment resistance is not just a symptom of biological illness, nor simply the re-enactment of painful experience. It can also be understood as a communication—and, thus, as a sign of hope—that someone will help them understand their experiences *and* hold them accountable for their actions. With perspective and accountability, these patients as adults might no longer have to contort themselves to fit a mismatched environment, but instead face the limitations in themselves and others in order to negotiate a better fit, using their adult authority. This is a basic piece of learning for any mature citizen.

In any treatment system, staff and other patients are inevitably caught up in each patient's powerful affective communications and induced through projective identification to react to and relive with the patient the essence of the patient's authority struggles. In fact, the interactive struggles of individuals who bring with them irrational family roles are embedded in all forms of social (and political) interaction. Riggs patients and their treatment process illuminate aspects of these difficulties, outlining the background for some of the most intractable political problems of contemporary society. Riggs' mission, with its focus on authority, is a lens for examining this process.

Taking charge

To get beyond crises, many of these patients need a longer-term relationship with clinicians within a focused system that includes psychopharmacologic treatment but goes beyond it. Such a system provides a working framework for specially trained clinicians who can tolerate these patients' difficult personalities and their negative reactions to authority long enough to help them see themselves more clearly, translate behavioral communications into language, learn how and why they have shaped themselves in a particular way, put their lives in historical perspective, and help them reshape how they deal with their interpersonal world.

In the course of their development, these patients may have discovered that the only way they can feel in charge is to resist caregivers—voices of authority whom they have often experienced as untrustworthy. A global antipathy to authority can be a limiting factor for those who might otherwise engage more fully as citizens. This resistance happens sometimes only internally and passively but for our patients can contribute to a chaotic interpersonal process which not infrequently gets played out in relationships outside of the treatment. Since these patients may not have developed language to describe their painful experiences, an outpatient therapist who necessarily stands at a distance from the patient's behavior often can't discern what is happening in the patient's outside world or help contain the impact of behavior long enough to make sense of it within the therapeutic relationship. Riggs provides a larger human system—a community—where patients are invited to engage with other patients and staff within a containing institutional framework designed for learning. It is this framework and the treatment task that makes Riggs a laboratory for learning about the systems psychodynamics of citizenship.

Because Riggs is a voluntary, hospital-based continuum of care, there are myriad opportunities for patients to develop a range of relationships; they participate in shaping their own treatment rather than simply complying with a staff design. When their behavior evokes irritation in others and they experience themselves as victims, others are available to help them notice their own responsibility, both social and political. The freedom of the open setting coupled with a commitment to examining the meaning of what happens in that setting makes their choices more visible, opening an opportunity for patients to see their own role in creating painful repetitions.

Unpacking our patients' communications reveals that unconscious and historically based images of the self in relation to a parent become enacted through projective identification and are then carried by other patients and staff. Negative staff reactions to the patient and between staff members, when studied in the context of the treatment task, can be understood as aspects of countertransference evoked by the patient's communications (E. R. Shapiro & Carr, 1987). Placed in historical perspective, these relationships can be understood as unconscious attempts by patients to replicate and learn about their problematic earlier experiences.

> To illustrate how this works, consider Jennifer who experienced her male therapist as empathic, responsive, available, and good. This was in stark contrast to her experience of her female nursing care coordinator, whom she found harsh, unforgiving, unavailable, and inconsiderate, an experience that justified Jennifer's angry treatment of her. The therapist, who did not experience the nurse so harshly, noted that Jennifer was presenting split, polarized transference views of her caregivers, where she was keeping her therapist in her mind as all "good" and the nursing staff member as "bad."

> To help her begin to recognize her use of splitting, he pointed out that, as her therapist, he was in charge of her treatment and, therefore, the nursing care was something that he was overseeing. He wondered about the patient's difficulty in holding him accountable for the nursing provision and raised the possibility that the patient was preserving him in an idealized space in her mind. Further exploration revealed that this preservation of an idealized parent was a defensive structure derived from Jennifer's childhood experience. Recognizing this was the first step in Jennifer's development of a capacity to hold both loving and angry feelings for the therapist in her mind in order to gain a new perspective on past family relationships.

To facilitate the development, containment, integration, and interpretation of the patient's range of relationships, the therapist who is providing the intensive individual psychotherapy is a member of an interdisciplinary team. While holding onto a perspective of the patient's mind, the therapist and the team leader each take up a consultative role to the team's process. They listen to the intense relationships the patient develops with other patients and staff members and consider them as potentially split-off aspects of the developing focal relationship with the therapist. The team leader endeavors to help team members unpack and understand how the team process is illuminated by the patient's history and struggles. The therapist explores with the patient what keeps the patient from focusing these enacted internal images into the relationship with him.

> For example, a team leader found himself increasingly irritated at and critical of the social worker's "endless worries" about Sam's missed appointments with her. The therapist called the team leader's irritation to his attention, noting that the tension between the team leader and the social worker mirrored the split relationship between Sam's parents, where mother "worried" obsessively and father criticized her.

This is an example of leadership from below (see Chapter Nine). The team leader was caught up in a problematic relationship. The therapist, a team member, took up a leadership role by clarifying the *relatedness* of the clinical pair to the task of treatment; team members and the team leader could follow his lead and further develop that insight.

The parents—and now the team members—were having trouble functioning as a working pair in holding Sam accountable. The perspective offered by the discussion allowed the therapist to begin an exploration with Sam of his anger and grief about the inability of his parents to work together and provided an opportunity to help the parents (and the team members) to see the meaning and consequences of their stereotyped argument.

This is what we all do: We play out our earlier relationships through our engagement with society—and society is large enough for us to find compliant others to take up the unconsciously determined roles that we need for our emotional stability. Within the framework provided by this institution, however, the primary task, our roles, and an interpretive stance provide opportunities to use those experiences for learning.

Another arena for displacement of transference feelings at Riggs is in relationships between patients. The staff discourage exclusive relationships between patients for a number of important reasons, one of which is the risk of emptying the individual therapy of meaning. An exclusive pair of patients challenges the therapist–patient pair's focus on the unfolding transference. Feelings that might otherwise have been brought into the treatment are readily displaced into the patient pair and enacted there without interpretation.

> For example, as a child, Laura was sexually abused by a babysitter and was beginning to bring into her therapy her rage at her parents for not noticing the abuse and not protecting her. She developed an intense relationship with another patient, whom she continually verbally abused. Neither patient spoke to their therapist about this tension-filled relationship, but nursing staff noticed it. When the team began to perceive this shared enactment of childhood abuse (with roles reversed), the therapist could help Laura notice the way she kept the therapist (as parent) from the necessary information he needed to help her. This observation allowed Laura to consider the many assumptions she had about her parents as a child, which had inhibited her ability to turn to them for help.

These examples cast in bold relief the myriad ways that we all unconsciously participate in creating the world around us. The repetitive quality of the relationships derived from our early experiences can cloud our capacity to take full authority for our participation. The Riggs example illuminates the kind of containment that may be necessary in order to make such blind spots more visible. Such containment is not confined to a psychiatric institution but is an aspect of all organizations when they are clear about their task and their members are authorized and invited to use their experience, listen to how the other may be right, and develop collaborative and task-related interpretations. Such an interpretive capacity can deepen individuals' engagement in any institution. To achieve such a capacity, however, the system must be managed.

Managing the system

Any institution comprises many boundaries: between roles, tasks, disciplines, levels of authority, between the working organization and its board, and between the institution and the outer society. Each of these boundaries must be managed, in terms both of concrete structures (policies and procedures) and of efforts to make sense of what transpires across them (interpretation). Such interpretation takes place in many forms and in different disciplinary languages in every institution.

In this treatment institution, everything becomes relevant to the primary task of helping patients take charge of their communications, their affectively charged eruptions, and their lives. Arnold Modell (1975, 1984), a psychoanalyst who worked with very troubled patients, described how all human beings are "open systems joined by the means of communication of affects." How this communication functions and how it can best be used therapeutically becomes a central question for a clinical system. Affectively charged communications are the unmanaged center of our patients' psychological difficulties. Negotiating boundaries in which the dialogue embedded in these communications and split relationships can be heard, withstood, and translated is a central aspect of an interpretive treatment. Given this unremitting focus at Riggs, the need for containing boundaries for interpretation runs throughout the institution. Powerful affective communications are addressed at multiple boundaries in dyads, small and large groups, and as a total system. Managing the system can be understood as negotiating a series of task boundaries.

> For example, a housekeeper erupts in anger at her supervisor. The supervisor places her on warning for insubordination. Such an event raises a question for any system attending to systems psychodynamics. Might such

an incident be considered as a communication from the system, as in the lunchtime sitting arrangement of the senior staff that I described in Chapter Nine?

After review, it becomes clear that the eruption followed the housekeeper's spending three hours cleaning up vomit in public bathrooms shared by patients. Competent management of this event requires developing a range of questions. For example, is this just an irritable employee who needs to learn to manage her feelings at work? Is this an employee eruption that is symptomatic of an oppressive authority structure where the staff's work and commitment are not adequately recognized? Or, more clinically, has the patient community unwittingly "selected" a particular patient to vomit on the staff's building as an angry way to communicate their wish that the caregivers take more notice of their anger? Is the vomit a statement from patients that the staff's "food" is indigestible? Have they pushed a particular staff member to express anger on their behalf? Deciding which of these and other questions to explore becomes the task of the system. Given this complexity and the need to negotiate an interpretation, any premature certainty about which interpretive response is accurate would be evidence of trouble in the system and a contribution to the creation of irrational roles and a loss of task focus.

Generally, the patients at Riggs represent and re-enact difficult stories: the rage of past generations of suffering, the inability to look directly at the ways we damage our children, the sexual exploitation of the innocent in the service of past hurts. Our patients are messengers of truths that society cannot bear to see and learn from; our institutional task is to help translate these truths into a language that can be grasped both by the patient and the social surround (Elmendorf & Parish, 2007).

In all institutions, subgroups have different roles, managing differentiated aspects of the task. Interpretive work—and careful management—are necessary to refine the task connections for each group. For example, psychiatric residential treatment is expensive. Riggs' business staff focus on effective financial management. But the institutional mission is about helping our patients to be in charge. Though helping patients and their families to effectively manage the costs is connected to this mission, the families' feelings about the cost and the meaning of this resource can get in the way, requiring the clinical perspective.

At Riggs, patients and their families are inevitably confronted with the limitations of financial resources. Their feelings about the meaning of these resources can make it hard for them to think clearly about how to manage them. This is true whether the resources are derived from college funds, retirement funds, family resources, or insurance. As I've indicated, business and clinical staff together meet with patients and families to integrate both approaches: What are the facts of the limitations and what feelings are involved in decisions about how to use resources?

> This happened for Sam, whose parents wanted to support his treatment and took money out of their retirement accounts. Sam felt both in need of his parents' support and guilty about taking limited resources. In response to his guilt, he requested to step down to a less costly program at Riggs, but his clinical status required more intensive nursing care than the step-down program provided. His stress was thus multiply determined, but his proposed solution (to step down) was a managerial rather than an interpretive effort. In part, Sam's suicidal feelings were related to his guilt about being the cause of family stress. His parents also felt guilty because of their recognition that their own limited emotional availability contributed to Sam's difficulties. They tried their best, however, to provide the necessary financial resources. No family member was able to think clearly about this situation because "limited resources" was a notion that referred both to a concrete financial reality and metaphorically to emotional availability. In the absence of clarification of the concrete and metaphorical meanings of the cost of treatment, family members were inevitably unclear about which one they were discussing.

The team of business staff and clinicians reviews these kinds of issues and helps members of the treatment team bring them into the family work to support a conversation in which the actual finances are grasped, realistic needs laid out, and emotional conflicts articulated. This negotiation, where everyone's needs and limitations—both financial and emotional—can be faced and a new solution reached, is a crucial aspect of treatment. Ultimately, Sam did step down, but his program shift was related to his clinical improvement based on the additional perspective he and his family had developed about their guilty feelings, their shared history, and their new understanding about the emotional meaning of limitations. One outcome of bringing these subgroups in the institution together to maximize their differentiated links to the institution's task was a deepening of engagement in each role: business staff, clinical staff, patients, and families.

So, what is the relevance of all of this to the citizen role? Riggs offers a model of organizational containment in a learning institution with a particular task. Society, in its general sense, provides neither containment nor focus. Institutions do. Though all of us bring our irrational roles from our families into our organizations, once we join an institution in a role that is shaped by the institution's task, we begin to have containers in the mind for the mutual examination of experience. In a self-reflective institution, *relationships* can be linked to staff's *relatedness* to the mission. The collective use of the interpretive stance will support the possibility of using painful or difficult feelings, not in the service of blaming other people or the system, but as opportunities to learn together about the way the institution is carrying out its mission (see Chapters Three and Four). Deepening that collective staff learning facilitates the use of the mission as a lens onto the outer society.

For Riggs, the mission is about helping so-called "treatment resistant" patients become people taking charge of their lives. This mission focuses on helping people to shift out of irrational roles that have emerged in their families. In addition, it focuses on authority: taking charge. This focus and the discipline of listening for how the other may be right can cut across the projective use of others as containers for bits of our experience that we find difficult to bear or learn from. This opens opportunities for claiming more task-related roles and a deeper participation in a shared mission, a building block of competent citizenship. In Riggs' case, as I will illustrate in Chapter Twelve, this has allowed staff members (and some patients) to take up public voices around issues of public policy, education, child-rearing, and citizenship, taking a stand with the authority derived from their institutional experience and task perspective.

CHAPTER ELEVEN

Derailment and Recalibration of the Mission

Institutions, like people, periodically lose their way. Rapidly changing aspects of both the inner and outer worlds of institutional life can contribute to a loss of mission focus. Regaining the orienting connection to society in a way that enhances the work of the organization, better integrates the staff as a community, and sharpens the mission lens to the outside not infrequently requires outside help. Because an institution's mission is its link to the outside world, recalibration of that mission inevitably involves learning on behalf of society (E. R. Shapiro, 2013).

In this chapter, I will explore two examples of derailment in the mission of Riggs that ultimately illuminated two issues: differentiation/integration and autonomy/dependency. Within any political system, differentiation of roles and delegation of authority pulls at the capacity for any member to feel part of an integrated community. If you get more authority, does it necessarily diminish me? And, if I feel diminished by your advancement because it feels like you have more power and I have less, is it possible for you to listen to how I am right? Might I be seeing the ways your advancement has not been on behalf of a shared mission?

A second and related political tension is between dependency and autonomy. Some of this tension is represented in America by the two-party system, where the Democratic party focuses on the needs of the community and the Republican party on the autonomy of the individual. When these become polarized, the learning about the integration of the two that is necessary for social development can be derailed (see Chapter Thirteen).

The mission

Individuals, small groups, and organizations are all open systems, linked by the communication of affects (Modell, 1984). They all share a single characteristic: an internal world, an external world, and a boundary function that links the two. For an organization, the primary task (the mission) serves as the central boundary function; it is negotiated between the organization and the outside world and links the organization's survival to the needs of the larger society. A clearly negotiated mission is, therefore, a prime representation of interdependency. The mission authorizes and energizes the work of participants in the organization's internal world and is a marker of the organization's efforts to grapple with reality. It is a container for staff feelings and commitments and for their affective engagement with the world; it is a stabilizing force in the face of organizational regression, and it is a lens onto the outside world (E. R. Shapiro, 2004, 2005). The ways the staff sets up its authority configurations should optimize mission-related work.

Organizations develop through processes of increasing differentiation and integration as they come into contact with challenges from the internal and external world. Certain challenges—for particular missions—can lead to derailments of organizational development. Given the central boundary function of the mission, its character and shape can serve not only as a lens onto society but a means through which to grasp organizational vulnerabilities. As I indicated in earlier chapters, when the mission is clearly negotiated (taking into account the institution's resources, history, traditions, and commitments) both internally and across the outer boundary, staff members can increasingly find their work commitments tied to a transcendent reference: something beyond themselves that contains a set of ideals, values, and beliefs. This set of commitments meets the staff's need for their work to have a larger significance and links them to discernible sets of social values.

At times of trouble, outside consultation can serve as a frame to contain a discussion long enough for the staff to grasp the problem, trace it to vulnerabilities inherent in the organization's mission, and allow the organization's internal processes to re-establish an unfolding developmental course. Such periodic consultations bring in the outside world. If consultants are working from an interpretive stance, they may be able to find the staff's work, study the various roles, and help re-establish links to the mission.

At Riggs, we had learned that for patients to transform their rigid personality defenses someone had to listen carefully in order to help them see what they could not recognize in themselves. As it turned out, this kind of rigidity was not confined to our patients. Transforming a traditional psychoanalytic institution into a more flexible structure was difficult; when we ran into trouble, our institution needed an outside perspective.

Inviting external consultation is a daunting prospect for a chief executive officer and senior administrative staff. Opening the institution for scrutiny requires confidence in consultants and staff, readiness to face challenges to personal and institutional narcissism, recognition of vulnerability and potential disruption in the face of outside perspectives, and a collective willingness to learn. Dynamic systems consultation can clarify how an organization is functioning, illuminating impasses in development.

Over the twenty years between 1991 and 2011, Riggs had multiple consultations. I will focus on two of them, ten years apart. I have selected these because the ideas may have application to other organizations. Focusing on affective communication across role boundaries and the relation of internal organizational structure to the mission, the first consultation clarified the tension between differentiation and integration, the second illuminated the inextricable link between dependence and autonomy.

Internal organizational structure: the blindness of power

As I indicated in Chapter Nine, in my effort to locate authority and shift the Riggs system from large to small group process, I reorganized the clinical staff into multidisciplinary teams with team leaders and created an executive committee consisting of nursing, operations, marketing, and the four senior medical staff team leaders, each of whom had multiple administrative roles. The executive committee met weekly for two hours. Over time, all members learned to grasp the whole institution by connecting their work to the work of their colleagues. As we learned together, the developing system became more manageable: links between marketing and admissions, between the therapeutic community and the psychotherapy, between the patient and staff communities became clearer—and the organization of the clinical work became more focused.

The executive committee came to love its work; our financial position improved, Riggs became more recognizable in the outside world, and the board was happy. But increasingly, the morale of the clinical staff plummeted. Though we listened to the staff, we could not figure out what was happening; we were doing well as an institution, but our colleagues were unsatisfied. We were losing our sense of an integrated community. Following discussions with the board, we decided to get an external consultation. Our consultants interviewed members of the clinical and administrative staff, both individually and collectively. Their exploration revealed that the unhappiness was primarily located in the next level of medical staff and the fellows (six post-residency psychiatrists and post-doctoral psychologists in training at Riggs for four-year periods). We had adjusted to the outside world, but our internal world was in disarray. Our new senior administration, our developing approach to marketing, litigation threats from families of very troubled patients, and the increasing external pressures of accreditation and outreach had shifted the organizational culture. The treatment program, founded on mutual trust and confidence, professional respect, sharing of information, and collaboration between clinical systems was facing a new and more differentiated organizational structure that increasingly brought the outside world into view. The new "corporate mentality" was experienced by clinical staff as alien and disruptive.

Clinical staff members were feeling abandoned and unrecognized by management. They were losing their picture of the institution and felt an unfamiliar lack of excitement in their work. Staff members had reactions to my new CEO title, which the board had added to facilitate easier communication with related organizations but which seemed to be taking priority in the minds of the staff over my functioning as their medical director. They felt we had introduced a newly commercial, line-management approach. The previous sense of collegial collaboration had been transformed into public conversations about "reporting to managers and directors."

We had also created the Erikson Institute to focus on clinical research and education (Fromm, 2006, 2011; Mintz, 2002; Muller & Tillman, 2007; Perry et al., 2009; Plakun, 2011). But this gave staff members the feeling that their medical director was de-emphasizing the centrality of the therapy and the therapeutic community program. My enthusiasm for the developing and expanding institution felt to them like an exercise of power rather than work being carried out on their behalf. As such, a hierarchical feel dominated the institution. Meetings had taken on a new language: The words "report to" or "consult with" had taken over what used to be called "talking with." The four senior male clinicians and the medical director (all members of the executive committee) had become undifferentiated in the minds of the clinical staff. They referred to us in private as "The Blob." The voices of female leaders and administrators were not heard. The staff saw the executive committee as a black hole into which ideas and questions disappeared. Their experience was that they had to go to everyone and anyone in this group with questions—and that they inevitably got different answers.

Our consultants recommended that we work toward removing the line-management mentality in order to recover a sense of colleagueship. They pointed to the accretion of power in "The Blob" and recommended that these senior managers divest themselves of their multiple roles in order for others to share in overseeing the institution. They noticed that we had not authorized the next generation of staff to lead.

These observations took us by surprise. Our consultants had seen what we could not: Despite its successes, our new organizational structure had left the system feeling de-authorized and disenfranchised. Staff members reported that during the executive committee's weekly meetings, our laughter and banter could be heard through the door in the corridors. They felt that we were energized and having fun while they suffered. Unwittingly, we had formed an exclusive power group, self-satisfied about our work and smug about our effectiveness. As a leader, I had shifted the hierarchy toward small-group functioning, but had not sufficiently attended to the need for transparency, sentience, and recognition of the capacity and desire of the larger system to share responsibility for the institution's direction. I had failed to recognize the need for greater distribution of task-related authority.

After extended discussion, I decided to disband the executive committee, flattening the hierarchy and distributing leadership roles more broadly, involving younger members of the staff. I restructured the organization with a much smaller team of system leaders (nursing, clinical, community, finance, marketing, development, Erikson Institute) with whom I met individually, inviting each to take authority and responsibility for developing their areas under a defined set of policy guidelines. I formed a much larger coordinating committee (seventeen to twenty people), that met monthly for the purposes of sharing information, developing links with each other, and solving system problems. Members were free to invite their colleagues to meetings when they felt the agenda was relevant. We published our minutes and morale improved. In this transition, several issues stood out.

First, the executive committee did not give up its power easily; one member even told me, "You don't have the authority to do this!" Second, I had not recognized the extent of discussion and authorization from below that was necessary for major system change and systems integration. I had lost the picture of an integrated community. I began to see the ways in which broader discussion, more widely spread information, and openness to new ideas were necessary for collaborative change.

Following this reorganization, we formed a transition team to assess the impact of the changes. The group raised a number of questions to focus the staff's discussion. These included a focus on the redistribution of roles that had resulted from the reorganization which had left the staff with an experience of "winners." and "losers." Those not selected had taken the risk to apply and had to manage their grief, hurt, and anger. Among the "losers" were senior staff members, previously on the executive committee, who had lost their valued work group and the power of holding multiple roles. Could we shift the culture to one where individual contributions, in whatever role, could be recognized and valued? Could we use our collective experience of envy, competition, limited resources, loss, and injury through the interpretive stance to deepen our learning about the more painful experiences in our patients' lives?

The new structure had the medical director meeting individually with system heads, leading to a pairing dynamic. Could pairing be seen as bringing together differentiated competencies in the service of a task, or would it only be used as a focus for envy and feelings of exclusion? Could these issues be discussed openly? The reorganization invested authority in individual roles rather than a "blobbed" executive committee. Could the new leaders negotiate authority from below and maintain their differentiation from each other rather than being "blobbed"?

All of this is the data of systems psychodynamics (Armstrong, 2006; Fraher, 2004; Gould et al., 2006; Hirschhorn, 1990; Miller & Rice, 1967; Obholzer & Roberts, 1994; Rice, 1966; E. R. Shapiro & Carr, 1991; Wells, 1995). Since we knew that the working links between individuals, small groups, and the larger organization are revealed through the communication of affects, facing our painful feelings within multiple roles, taking them seriously as information, making them public, and listening to how these feelings reflected the workings of the system led us to collaboratively reorganize to maximize full engagement with the task.

Over time, the new organization appeared effective in improving morale. In particular, the coordinating committee began to reveal that our system consisted of multiple, newly differentiated voices, each with a distinctive perspective. The resultant open, lively discussion led to better authorization of system heads from below, more widespread integration, and a broader grasp of the institution and its potential for engagement in the world. In addition, the learning about the inevitable tensions between power and authority, between differentiation and integration sharpened all of our attention to these issues in our outside political world.

Dependency and autonomy

The second consultation, ten years later, came in the context of my announced retirement, the imminent retirement of the three male senior staff members, and some unusually intense clinical disruptions. One of the foci of Riggs treatment is to help its patients increasingly communicate in words what they have learned to communicate only through behavior. Though the center has a wide range of clinical resources, the freedom we give our patients carries with it some risk. Periodically, our patients get involved in self-destructive behavior, often involving the entire patient group. This can include drug use, sexual acting out, cutting, even suicide. While attending to the group and the individual patients involved, the clinical staff inevitably consider themselves: is there something the staff are doing or not paying enough attention to that the patients are trying to bring to our attention through this behavior?

It was in one of these moments that we decided to get outside consultation. Though we had already intensively reviewed the clinical disruptions—and brought in outside clinical and accrediting reviewers for their perspectives, we felt we needed more. On both internal and external review, our clinical procedures appeared to be competent and thorough. Significant self-destructive behavior in our system was an uncommon event—and over the years the incidents had been falling. Nonetheless, the staff were traumatized by the premature discharge of several longer-term patients after severe self-destructive behavior that challenged the system. We invited our consultants to examine our clinical system for blind spots. What were we not paying attention to that might in some way be contributing to the patients' and staff's disarray and demoralization?

Again, consultants interviewed a wide range of staff members, sat in on clinical reviews of patients, and sorted through our various documents about the system and the clinical issues. They were looking at the institution as a whole, searching for underlying dynamic system tensions. Their primary finding was that the vulnerability of the staff to the clinical disruptions—and some of the patients' behavior—might have more to do with the developing institution than with any specific areas of clinical inattention. They focused on the holding environment and issues of dependency.

In private interviews, staff members spoke to our consultants about the imminent retirement of the center's four most senior male clinicians, including the medical director/CEO. The crucial role of senior staff in maintaining the institution—and the experience they had accumulated through their multiple roles—had earned the respect but also the considerable dependency of younger staff. In addition, it had generated significant ambivalence, competition, and resentment. In the context of transition, the consultants found evidence of gaps between senior and junior clinical staff with "a sense of an absence of adequate nourishment." In addition to the inevitable isolation and trauma felt by those closest to the clinical disruptions, our consultants found a deep sense of loneliness and isolation in the generation of staff that was facing the imminent retirements. Beyond that, the prominence of these four men had contributed to an obscuring of women's voices and female authority.

The findings revealed that we were not listening to ourselves. The consultants discerned a peculiar bias in our listening: We were not attending to our own irrationality and dependency. Focusing on the stereotypic differences between "male" and "female," they outlined the distinctions between "paternal" and "maternal" voices in our organizational processes. In the clinical system, they felt the "paternal" voice was located in the therapeutic community program with its emphasis on rationality, boundaries, roles, and tasks—and the associated focus on reality. They located the "maternal" stance in the nursing staff, with their focused receptivity to maternal longings and dependency needs. Staff tensions they discerned between these two subsystems suggested that the organization was enacting an unconscious notion that dependency and autonomy—the maternal and paternal voices—were either/or positions. We had unwittingly failed to integrate the predominant affects in our subsystems with our mission; we were disconnected from each other.

They reminded us that patients and staff continually live with both. They suggested that our focus on patients' aggression might be obscuring our recognition that our patients' deeper maternal longings and wishes for merger and fusion were regularly present, increasingly obscured, and insufficiently addressed. In particular, we had not provided a contained space for staff and patients to review their feelings about the loss of significant patients through their premature terminations—or about the imminent loss of the senior staff.

In response, we reviewed the institution's clinical evolution and its mission. As I have indicated, the clinical mission of Riggs is to help "treatment resistant" patients become people taking charge of their lives. The tension between dependency and autonomy runs through the spectrum of treatment. In the initial phases, Riggs provides a twenty-four-hour nursing staff. We assign nursing care coordinators to meet regularly with each patient. These nursing staff members help patients take care of their bodies, their spaces, feelings, immediate needs, and stresses. As patients progress through their treatment, learning to use the intensive psychotherapy and to manage their own behavioral communications, they begin to move out through our continuum of care, attenuating their individual contacts with the nursing staff. Increasingly, the patients turn to groups for support, shifting toward the use of community staff, social workers, and others for help in moving out into the outside community.

As we increasingly defined the task of these programs, the nursing administration, in consultation with the rest of us, decided that the patients should end their relationship with the nursing care coordinator as they became more involved in the outside world. Though this limit made sense in terms of the patient's increasing autonomy and the need for managing staff time, it emerged in the consultation as an administrative symptom of a larger system-wide blind spot: we had not paid enough attention to the inextricably linked dynamics of dependency and autonomy.

As patients advance toward greater autonomy, their dependency needs and maternal longings are not necessarily reduced and still need to be met. We realized that our administrative termination of the relationship with their nurse had been arbitrary and un-negotiated. We had not trusted our patients to attenuate it in consultation with their nursing care coordinator, as the external support was no longer needed. We had not provided a contained setting for this.

Instead, we took over and de-authorized our patients' competence, losing sight of our mission. We were acting irrationally, as if we believed that "taking charge" meant no longer having dependency needs. Was this a symptom for the staff as well? What had distracted us from providing containers for mourning the endings of the senior clinicians, for supporting the administrative advances of the younger staff, for preparing for the arrival of new leadership, for the acknowledgement of interdependent relationships?

Discussion

The structures of authority in any institution become receptacles within which staff members locate their relatedness to the mission. Riggs had managed for decades with a much more generic mission involving a psychoanalytic approach to treatment. The institution organized power and authority at the top, with an individual psychoanalyst leader plus individual treatment. It was a familiar structure for a psychoanalytic institution, where the primary mission was individual psychoanalytic psychotherapy. Authority was located in "the psychoanalyst;" the rest of the clinical staff managed their work lives at some distance from the psychotherapy. But the world was changing and in order to sustain its mission the institution had to adapt its treatment focus on the individual to relate more to the family, the group, and the community.

For the staff, the new mission, negotiated when I first arrived, spoke to important values and beliefs: the significance of the individual life, sustaining the tension between the needs of the individual and the needs of the community, the importance of individual authority, and the centrality of relationships. The mission was a guidepost that could allow staff to reorient themselves when individual and group dynamics began to pull them into irrational functioning.

Opening the institution's boundaries to the new and unfamiliar had been necessary in order to creatively adapt and manage the future. It had led to increased staff differentiation, initially organized within the executive committee. We had been stuck at the next step: systems integration. With the benefit of an external perspective, our first consultation illuminated how the assignment of multiple roles to a few senior staff members had inadvertently disenfranchised the rest of the staff and increased their dependency. It pointed to our need for a broader, more integrated authority structure that used the staff's differential expertise to more fully engage our mission with the outer world. We were not holding the needs of both the individual and the community—one of our mission's central values—and our institution's development had been derailed.

The second consultation illuminated the ways we had lost touch with the need to meet the dependency inevitably mobilized at times of development, transition, and growth. We had forged ahead, creating new programs, developing our external voice, creating an educational and research institute—but we had not seen the ways we had disregarded irrational aspects of our work and bypassed the needs of those who were departing (both the retiring staff and the discharged patients) and those who remained. We were avoiding the pain of loss, and we were not seeing its clinical and organizational implications. We had been blind to the support people need in order to take charge of their lives. In both cases, the consultative perspective helped us to resume our organizational development.

Learning on behalf of society

How do these experiences and formulations apply to other organizations and to our larger society? The Riggs mission of helping patients to take charge of their lives contains issues of developmental impasse, irrationality, authority, dependency, and autonomy. These elements turned out to be foci for institutional derailment at particular points of institutional development. Every institution has similar issues and similar internal and external pressures that affect their staff's capacities to focus on the mission. These pressures can be grasped through institutional self-reflection and a leadership that listens, recognizes limitations, and, when necessary, seeks outside resources. These critical clarifications enhance an institution's capacity to use its mission as a lens into society.

With that sharpened lens, a number of political issues in our larger society immediately become apparent. Does our government focus on the integration of our communities around a shared mission or does it funnel power to selected groups? And when it does the latter, what is the cost of disenfranchisement? Do our collective support systems create excessive dependency in one area (e.g. the homeless) and excessive autonomy in another (e.g. the 1%)? What is required for the integration of these splits? When we recognize such issues through our institutional learning, we can begin to have an informed voice as citizens.

Part III

A Citizen in Society

To this point, I have outlined the transition from family to organizational membership and described the group and individual dynamics that comprise the joining process. I have outlined the link between organizational roles and the institution's primary task and pointed to the ways these tasks connect to the needs of the outside society, carrying social ideals and values. In my institutional example, I detailed the combination of interpretation and management necessary to maximize the potential use of the mission as a lens onto society.

In this section, I begin by describing one institution's interpretive reach into the larger society and explore how different organizational contexts interpret the same phenomena, offering an example of a collaborative interpretation of an aspect of society negotiated across institutional boundaries. Focusing on the United States, I then explore the possibility that nations, too, might have tasks on behalf of society. Through the study of two individuals, I bring these ideas together to illustrate how citizens might discover their authority to take a stand through an examination, interpretation, and synthesis of their memberships in groups and organizations.

In my final chapter, I propose that this systems-psychodynamic exploration of interpretive citizenship suggests a notion of society as a multicellular organism in the process of development. The interpretive stance then becomes a tool for maximizing the voices of citizens so that they can collectively join through their bounded entities in the further development of society.

CHAPTER TWELVE

Approaching Society through Institutions

As individuals, we join society and separate from it, feel its complexity and use our more familiar contexts to relate to it. But society is too vast to be used simply. Unlike psychology or theology, society is not a group or field that can be grasped. Each person must begin with a definite access point and consider the complexity of his or her unique perspective in order to negotiate any shared interpretation with others that moves toward a joint perspective as citizens.

Insofar as there are inevitable links between institutions and the wider society, it is possible to approach social interpretation through the lens of the institution's task. Our commitment to group membership derives from our family roles and multigenerational past—and enacts an aspect of society. The relationship is reciprocal; our groups and their engagement with others shape our understanding of society (Carr, 1993). Our various organizations are significant contexts—often unconscious and covert—that shape the way we experience the world. In this chapter, I explore two areas: an institution's mission engaging a larger social need and the possibility of developing a deeper understanding of society across institutional boundaries (Khaleelee, 1994; Khaleelee & Miller, 1985).

An institution responds to society's needs

One of the tasks of institutions is to provide the channels through which individuals and subgroups in a society interact and thus create the needed space between themselves as individuals and their vast contexts. One way to consider this is through the study of religious institutions (E. R. Shapiro, 2019) and their management of grief, both personal and societal.

Religious institutions deliberately acknowledge dependency though their belief in God, pastoral activities, and acts of worship. Like art, religious bodies acknowledge the irrational aspects of daily life without presuming that such aspects are pathological. Religion both affirms dependency (which society can devalue as "immature") and deals with profound emotions like fear, love, grief, guilt, and anxiety. The social task of religious institutions is, then, to help individuals to face the connections between their interdependency and their feelings about the transcendent by providing a managed and contained context for both (Carr, 1985).

Let me expand this idea for a moment. Religious institutions exist in the world—and the rest of us are aware of them, even if we don't pay attention to them. All the major monotheistic religions emphasize how the self is inextricably linked to the larger collective of humanity, resisting any excessive emphasis on the individual. With some link to this perspective, individuals can, even if only unconsciously, risk relaxing the boundary around themselves or around their exclusive subgroup in order to maximize their capacity to recognize that we are all equal members of the human community. In a globalized world with increasing numbers of refugees, this is a recognition that is increasingly in danger of being lost.

As I will illustrate, the rituals and symbols of religion, brought forth at significant moments, can facilitate a shared regression in which conflicted feelings and experiences around dependency and the search for transcendent meaning can be dealt with in a constructive rather than chaotic manner. *Regression* is a problematic word, since it can imply pathology. I use the term here to refer to a developmentally appropriate relaxation of the boundaries that sharply define us as separate individuals, leading to the possibility of an identification with others and with the larger society. This kind of joining requires a containing structure within which individuals can feel safe enough to allow both regression and joining. This is what religious institutions, with their traditions, rituals, and history, can provide.

Wesley Carr suggested that both the activity of church members and the unconscious relatedness of those in the outside world to religious institutions can facilitate a general social regression away from isolation and toward interdependency in the service of society's development and its survival. He noted that religious services are held even when no one attends. It is important, he believed, that members of the larger society know that the services are always available—and that the connection to the transcendent continues to exist somewhere. Services are held "on behalf of" the rest of us.

How is such societal influence transmitted in religious institutions? First, there are the ritualized affirmations of the transitions—or what Wesley called the "ultimate boundaries"—of life, including the entry into the world and the exit from it. Rituals are linking phenomena that allow for the recognition of connections to the past, to cultural heritages, and to the significant developmental transitions (birth, adolescence, marriage, and death). For believers and unbelievers alike, such rituals allow for constructive regression and joining, furthering the development of the participants. I wonder whether our increasing secularization of these rituals has contributed to moving too many of us away from this kind of transcendent integration across differences.

The second major area for religious ritual is in the service of public events, particularly those involving death. For example, in the national service in London managed by religious leaders after the Falklands victory in 1982, the service needed to attend in a more complex way than the simplistic victory that was expressed by political leaders. Conflicting feelings of rage, grief, jubilation, horror, and vindictiveness divided the country. Within the public ritualized celebration, religious spokespeople could offer a more complex, linking interpretation that allowed for the integration of disparate groups. In their identification with this linking interpretation, individuals could regress and shift out of their highly differentiated, often narcissistically invested and conflicting positions, into a more unified identification with a complex society.

In another example, with the same task but in a very different setting, Wesley's design for the funeral of Diana, Princess of Wales, incorporated history, diverse culture, and contemporary symbols that transcended national, religious, and cultural boundaries allowing millions of people around the world to join. The outcome of this event offered an opportunity to the larger society to engage the integrated private and social significance of mourning. Prior to his death, Wesley gave me a description of Diana's funeral:

> In 1997 Diana, Princess of Wales, was killed in a car accident in France. The funeral in Westminster Abbey was the Dean's responsibility. The event demonstrated the way an institution can function on a dynamic level on behalf of society. The funeral of Diana would be an opportunity for public symbolism. But of what kind?
>
> Diana initially presented herself to the public as an innocent youth. Her marriage to Prince Charles was attended by the international media, drawing worldwide attention with all of its pomp and ceremony as a "fairy-tale marriage". She represented hope, youth, beauty, and the next generation, not only in terms of her wished for role as the mother of the future king but also as a representative herself of the younger generation. This had particular significance for a monarchy whose leader had not changed since 1952. For forty-five years, there had been no collective public grieving.
>
> In her early marriage to Prince Charles, Diana was seen as the "Queen of Hearts". She gave birth to the future king, toured the world and displayed a wide interest in issues ranging from fashion to schools in impoverished neighbourhoods to bombs and mines. With her subsequent marital difficulties, she evoked connections to the next generation and the marital disarray and generational sexual dilemmas that are worldwide. Diana had strong symbolic connections to the Queen. The relationship was between the longest serving member of the monarchy (the Queen) and the newest member, the Princess. Each married young (the Queen, at age 21, and Diana at age 20) and they each soon gave birth to the heir.
>
> Diana's death was both public and shocking. Chased by paparazzi and fleeing them in a car with her Arab lover, her car crashed in a tunnel. The Queen decided that the funeral would be held in Westminster Abbey, a place traditionally reserved for coronations and state funerals. The service brought together tradition with innovation. As with the Princess' life, we altered the form to include a wide range of music from Verdi to contemporary. We included her favourite performer (Elton John) singing and playing the piano—and an emotional personal reflection from Diana's brother.

The event was televised worldwide and millions across the globe watched. People wrote about their experiences. Numbers of books of condolences were left at St. James and Kensington Palaces. Across the UK most cathedrals and many town halls and parishes were also involved. The public demanded notebooks in which to write, recording much more than condolences. Though the books remain private, it was reported than many were personal essays, poems, or other sophisticated literature. Letters and messages were sent to the Abbey, arriving every day for almost five months. Almost without exception, they began by thanking us and picking up one aspect of the service. They then told a story, usually of a personal bereavement that they had not previously been able to tell anyone. These accounts went back not just a few months, but for some as many as twenty years. It was as if unresolved grief had remained dormant in their lives until this peculiarly public writing became possible. The narratives followed a pattern: effusive thanks for the service, and an account of an incident in life that the service had reminded them of, followed by gratitude that they now could live with their grief for the first time. What was happening?

In an extraordinary way, Diana's death brought together personal and civic loss. Thousands stood in line for hours in front of St. James' Palace and the Mall to get their chance to write. The Palace provided tables and chairs, allowing people to spend hours writing and resting. But there was no fighting over space or anything else. People were in a profound dependence: for many Diana had obviously represented hope—not just for themselves, but for the monarchy—and they were at a profound loss without her. The monarchy was handling institutional loss for and on behalf of millions.

People from many nations of the world were so affected by their grief, that they could not move from grief to mourning. The deceased princess was claimed by many as a personal friend. The connection was always the same: some years previously when they were children, they had met her and they could not understand that their previous meeting did not qualify them for a place at the funeral. The extraordinary worldwide manifestation of dependency caught people unprepared. Modern society is supposedly individualistic, materialistic, and largely not religious. At best people regard religion as a private affair. As the then Press Secretary to the Prime Minister famously put it, "We don't do God!" The emotional reactions, signs of genuine sorrow and use of religious institutions by millions of people who knew the princess only from the media were unexpected. And the grieving took large amounts of time from people's lives. Members of the public and many large organisations were able to manage themselves through a space that allowed mourning both of the loss of Diana and her public role. People mingled grief for Diana with mourning for their own family and friends. Millions of people used this public role—with all of its irrationalities and impulsiveness—to stand for aspects of their own lives in ways that surprised them. Religious symbols and rituals were surprisingly powerfully engaging the participation of many.

After Diana's death, a million bouquets of flowers were placed in London alone. Thousands burned candles, a typical religious symbol. Many had packs of cards from which they took the Queen of Hearts, a title which the princess had said she hoped might someday be hers. My colleagues and I talked with people outside the Abbey for days. We found ourselves in touch with people highly dependent and at a loss. But they had moved together in some sort of collective role in relation to the institutions of society, to a state of profound self-awareness: they seemed to know what they were doing and they felt determined. (E. R. Shapiro, 2019, pp. 108–109)

He also gave me an interpretation of the outcome:

Institutional loss is both of the person and the roles that she holds on behalf of others. When I lose her, I don't just lose the part of myself that I invested in her. I also lose a bit of the picture of the social institution that I carry in my mind. When this institutional image is affected by bereavement, something within us remains damaged, without a public ritual of some sort that allows the shared reintegration of a new institutional view. This phenomenon underlines the way that public roles are used on behalf of other more private motives—the two sides may need to be recognised and integrated for institutional and social completion of the bereavement process. It may be that public grieving makes possible a more complex space—related to others—for private grief. It may even be that grief is always both a private and public affair. In order for people to live through and transcend the experience of personal bereavement, they need institutions-in-the-mind that endorse or even authenticate such grief. The mourning of death in an institution or society may be the foundation of personal mourning. (ibid., pp. 109–110)

Wesley felt that religious institutions keep alive what he called "the ultimate illusion"—the notion of God—that can be used to contain destructive aggression. Churches themselves do not contain illusions; instead it is the act of professing God that has that function. He outlined the increasingly visible conflict between the individual's need for a dependable object and the contemporary assumption that belief in God is a delusion. He once suggested that one difference between a delusion and a genuine religious experience is that the latter brings you closer to people. In their focus on the other world—God, life after death, a spiritual dimension to existence—religious institutions represent for the larger society a major area of human life that many believe is irrational. Commitment to such notions, however, can support risk-taking and surrender to an ideal.

Working across institutional boundaries

Different institutional contexts provide contrasting and often disconnected perspectives. Individuals working from the perspective of their institutional missions inevitably bring those differing perspectives into how they listen.

Once there was a nine-year-old boy who was asked to write a piece on "flying":

> I was at the cemetery looking at my dad's tombstone when my father rose up from his grave. He touched me on the forehead and with that my shoulder blades started to grow. I began to sprout wings! I was so amazed that I fainted. When I woke up my father was carrying me up to the sky. I was so frightened that I might fall and die, or he might drop me … ahhhhhhh. He did—I'm falling. Why has my father betrayed me! Wait a second, I'm not falling, I am flying! My father shouts to me, "I gave you my gift and now I must go." I yelled back, "Wait!" But it was too late. He had returned to his grave, never to awaken again. I felt so sad that he couldn't stay with me, but I also knew that he had given me a wonderful gift. I was soaring above the treetops like a colossal, proud eagle. The wind was blowing against my face

> like it does when I ride my bike really fast. As I flew through a cloud, the raindrops seemed like bugs hitting the car windshield. I wiped my face off and did the backflip I've been practicing so hard in the swimming pool. That was so much easier to do in the air!
>
> I started to get hungry and I really didn't want to eat bird food, so I headed back to land. When I touched the ground, my wings disappeared! I soon discovered that if I wanted to fly all I had to do was whisper "Dad," and my wings would magically appear.

This boy was my son, Joshua, who was given the assignment in school. When he showed it to me, I was moved by the story and proud of his work, and I reacted with warmth and praise. But, knowing that children need an interpretation-free space to develop their own ideas, I did not tell him what I made of his story. I thought to myself, "Josh is a young boy with an older father. He is aware of his grandparents' recent deaths and the ravaging illness of his uncle. He is reflecting on what he will be left with after I die."

My wife had a different interpretation through both her professional role as a psychologist and her role of mother. She thought, "Josh is writing about his use of his father to separate from his mother (earth) and thinking about what he has taken in from his dad that will allow him to fly on his own." Grounded in the marital and parental roles within a family, these interpretations are complementary; each offers the other a reflection of their shared connection to their child.

I then sent the story to Wesley Carr, who wrote to Josh, telling him that he had used the story in a sermon at Westminster Abbey. Wesley's interpretation came as a theologian. Writing to me, he said, "Joshua's questions resonate with some of the dilemmas of the Christian tradition. If Christ rose from the dead at the resurrection, where does he go then? St John says that Christ returns to the Father. What interests me is how Josh begins at the tomb, revels in the freedom of expression by flying, but then finds that any serious taking-off in life is only possible as long as he remembers the magic and symbolic word, 'Dad'. Josh recognizes that his father is a separate person and can die. But he also sees that his father can both be gone forever and invoked through his symbolic word. Any faith has to deal with the presence and absence of God at the same time. The capacity to locate the dead person in the mind is essential in handling bereavement; the loved one must be discovered as both present and absent. The strength of Josh's paper was that he understood the power of the internalized dead father."

Here is one small text, with three widely divergent interpretations, each of which reflects the differing institutional contexts the three of us carry. The interpreters share something in common; all three are embedded in a larger social structure. Our themes included anxiety about loss, the use of "the father" in managing separation, and the complexity and recognition of limits necessary for living and believing. These themes are at the same time divergent, linked, interesting, and insufficient. Did our differing interpretations join to something larger? I think not—they are simply contrasting interpretations of a child that derive from the perspective of different contexts. They were not offered in response to an external social need that pulled for the use of an institutional lens. There was no social question here to be explored; the learning was individual. Using the lenses of institutional missions to begin to make sense of the larger society must necessarily take a different course.

Interpreting society from linked institutions

As a psychoanalyst and director of a psychodynamic hospital, my work attends to the individual and his or her relations to the family and the community. To do this, I need to employ an interpretive stance within my institution both as a way to help the system mobilize itself, and to make some assessment of the relevant boundaries in the larger world so as to position my institution more broadly. But how does such an institution and its primary task relate to the larger society? How is it engaged with what's outside? And, when negotiating complex interpretations with other institutions, what learning does the outside world give back? The institution gives us a lens, a tradition, and mission-related authority to begin to make sense of aspects of the larger society. A respectful negotiation protects any one of us from claiming certainty about our perceptions of the outside world yet encourages us to still interact with that world.

Once, after an educational conference for clinicians at Austen Riggs on the theme of examined living, a request came from a local college to host a meeting of college counseling centers. They were noticing that a large proportion of the entering students were taking psychoactive medication and insisting that the counseling centers continue providing it. Moreover, students were requesting these medications for normal developmental experiences: failed love relations, exam anxiety, and so on. Counseling center staff members sensed that the students' turn to medication and drugs was adversely affecting their colleges' mission of learning, by substituting *managing* life for *learning* from it. Riggs seemed to them like an appropriate place outside of the counseling center world to bring the colleges together.

We agreed to the conference and a dozen colleges and universities sent representatives. We designed a retreat, enlisted counseling staff in presenting their experiences, and consulted from our position as members of a "community of examined living." Gradually, through four annual meetings, counseling center staff began to realize that they were taking up a particular kind of work on behalf of the larger educational system. Some had previously imagined that they had been doing a private practice, disconnected from the larger institution, until they began to see more clearly that this mindset was a defensive structure. This allowed them to begin to discern the pressures coming at them from both the university and the larger society that were mandating against treatment and toward management (Fromm, 2007).

Out of these discussions came the following negotiated interpretation from the perspectives of Riggs' mission and that of the colleges about child-rearing in American society:

> Over half of American marriages end in divorce, resulting in less social and psychological containment for children. Society has developed psychopharmacologic containment instead. When children go off to college, many have not developed sufficient emotional maturity in their families to manage the separation, and the family is less available to them because of its fragmentation. Parents, guilty about not taking good enough care of their children, expect the colleges to continue a parental role, and they hold the college accountable. But colleges, fearful of litigation and trying to recover their primary task of education, have moved away from the parental role. They now provide even less containment than formerly, with co-ed dormitories, no on-site adult supervision, and few restrictions. Colleges then enact the conflict by both turning to their college health services to provide parenting and decreasing the financial resources to support it. So, for example, college health services used to be a place where students could sleep overnight if they were excessively intoxicated. Some colleges have cut finances so that such services are no longer available. As a consequence, if a student is intoxicated, it becomes a matter for the police. The police then take over developmental containment in place of families and educational institutions. This observation raised a larger question about society: Are there similar

sequences in our society where previously sustaining institutions have lost their developmental function and begun managing our citizens instead of supporting them?

This complex interpretation emerged from discussions across institutional and role boundaries carried out by people from different organizations with related tasks and grounded in cross-validating interpretations. Recognizing that in this limited interpretive effort we had not attended to crucial input from families, students, police, and other stakeholders in these social dilemmas, we brought our initial collaborative view of this aspect of the larger society back into our institutions for further work, since the issues raised seemed congruent to the tasks of all.

Discussion

If we consider the escalating pressures on us, beginning with the intimate group of the family from which we have to differentiate, and add the forces coming from our group and institutional memberships and the chaotic pressures of the larger society, we can see how hard it is for any of us to find a space to think. However, if as individuals we develop an interpretive perspective from an institutional context that links to society's needs, a pathway to a citizen voice begins to emerge.

It may be that an attempt to understand society is a defense against the experience of despair about the world, a grandiose effort to manage the unmanageable. But some effort to make sense of the ungraspable by using our more familiar contexts as holding places may nonetheless be essential for psychological survival. A crucial aspect is whether we can work with others in such a way that they are led on to something new and original without really knowing why. Once we begin to work across institutions, the possibility of making sense of the next bounded entity—the nation—can emerge.

CHAPTER THIRTEEN

Do Nations Have Missions? American Identity

While institutional role and mission and the development of an interpretive stance are the first contexts for social interpretation, the next step toward finding the citizen voice requires focusing within the boundaries of nations. Searching for those boundaries raises the question about whether there is such a thing as a national identity and a national mission that addresses the origins and history of its citizens and connects to the needs of the global society. The tumultuous politics of the last two decades, the forming and dissolution of international collectives, and the recent pull toward nationalism has brought that question to the fore in the United States.

Let's go back a bit. During the chaotic presidential election of 2000 between George Bush and Al Gore, Americans witnessed a remarkably precise political polarization and an unprecedented politicization of the judiciary to solve a political impasse. In addition, there appeared to be systematic interference with voting in ethnic and lower income areas. The split vote in that year divided the country in half. For the first time, the political map presented on newscasts lucidly illustrated this political division by delineating in red the Republican center of the country and, in blue, the Democratic coastlines. In this map, I saw a split national identity where America's outer boundaries (at the ethnically diverse edges of our country) were liberally opening for contact with the outside world, while its internal life remained conservatively stable. It reflected a picture of national, political, and internal tension, with the center of the country holding a set of traditional Republican values about the importance of the individual (conservatism) and the outer boundaries illuminating the Democratic value of a differentiated community (liberalism). It seemed to me as though the pressures of outside influences were leading America at its boundaries to renegotiate its national identity, putting pressure on its internal sense of stability and familiarity.

Identity

Erik Erikson defined identity as developing congruence between a person's internal view of the self and the views of that self coming from others (Erikson, 1956; E. R. Shapiro & Fromm, 1999). Identity formation is a developmental step in adolescence, negotiated through relationships with others as the adolescent's body changes and the child begins to individuate from the family, undertaking a more mature role in a larger community of adults. Impediments to taking up an adult role can include reluctance to give up certainty (E. R. Shapiro, 1982a), intolerance of ambivalence and complexity, hatred of difference, projection of limitations, and other developmentally induced rigidities. A successful negotiation of identity requires a painful modification of the adolescent's narcissism. Beginning to recognize one's self in the less than idealized reactions of others signifies a step toward maturity and strengthens the capacity for flexibly grasping the realities of the larger world with their complexities and limitations.

Erikson's formulation about identity formation can be applied to nations which negotiate and renegotiate their identity both between their citizens and across their borders. A mature identity would incorporate an increasing congruence between internal and external views and include mature openness to complexity, increasing tolerance of differences, and acceptance of limitations. Such a maturing identity would result in a modification of national narcissism and strengthen the capacity for flexibly grasping the realities of the global community.

A review of the 1996 and 2000 presidential elections and the terrorist attacks of September 11, 2001 suggested to me the presence of a national struggle within the citizenry about grasping an American identity in transformation. Changes in the world were pushing Americans to give up a narcissistic position of moral superiority and move beyond subgroup identifications in order to find themselves as Americans in an increasingly global society and claim a more integrated role in the larger world. The subsequent elections of Barack Obama and Donald Trump suggest that these issues are far from resolved.

Prior to the national election of 1996, I participated in a large study of unaffiliated voters for the Center for National Policy in Washington (Center for National Policy, 1996; E. R. Shapiro, 2000b). Unaffiliated voters are those without clear party identifications. Their political significance lies in the recognition that their votes inevitably determine the election. As a group, unaffiliated voters illuminate issues that affect both parties and thus allow access to significant national trends. Psychologically, they are the leading edge of America's identity-in-formation.

In addition to extensive group interviews, I spoke with randomly selected voters from across the country. These people, from all ethnic groups, were feeling a loss of shared values. They talked passionately of the weakened sense of community, a breakdown of rules, and a view of America as "rudderless," without clear goals, direction, or a sense of vision. In a post-Cold War world where information technology, 24-hour media coverage, economic globalization, and the presence of powerful multinational corporations were blurring national boundaries, people could not effectively discover a larger context that allowed them to link their experiences and values to those of other Americans in passionate, meaningful commitments. Beyond the familiar structures of their own family and church, and their untested but strongly experienced membership in ethnic subgroups, they could discern no larger framework within which they could claim membership. Their grasp of the larger social scene was obscured by social turbulence, economic insecurity, gender and racial tensions, and political disenfranchisement and disaffection. They spoke of a "loss of authority" in the country and resultant anxiety and uncertainty about the future. There was a widespread feeling that "life is not as it should be." Many talked about feeling disconnected from wider social and political contexts, as if they were "all alone," "voiceless," or just "numbers" in a "political game" in which they simply did not count.

The voters had great difficulty articulating what America "stood for," although they were quite able to describe what it used to stand for. This feeling, I believe, was a backdrop for Trump's successful "Make America Great Again" politics in 2016. These voters could not identify core American values and beliefs. They were unsure of how to identify themselves in relation to others in a global community, and whether they could think of themselves as Americans or only in terms of their ethnic/racial/religious group. In the absence of an external context, ethnicity emerged as a binding framework that individuals could join.

Though ethnic identifications frequently emerge in subgroups of white Americans, I am using the term here to refer to those whom whites characteristically think of as "people of color," ranging from Native Americans to African Americans, Latinos, Hispanics, Asians, and the more recent Muslim immigrants from the Near East. Ethnic identifications brought these people together with others, linked them in a shared history that often included social trauma, and provided a framework for shared beliefs and values. For some, ethnic identifications offered a way of managing social projections.

For example, Frank was a single, thirty-eight-year-old African American waiter. He wanted to "diversify his skill set" but knew there was no job security in waiting tables and he had no hopes for a management position. "If a black man represents the restaurant," he said, "the customers get scared. ... Talent is not seen. You are black first." Frank was adamant about social issues but didn't feel that there was any clear source of power other than a general oppression. "Parents are working; the streets are raising the kids. Teachers are not paid enough to teach, so they don't care what kind of values they teach."

Frank's internal world, like that of many people I interviewed, was organized around his ethnic identifications. He did not experience himself as an individual American struggling with diverse opportunities and complex constraints. Instead, he located his experience within the imagined context of other African Americans who, he believed, passionately and deeply shared his picture of the ethnically oriented social world around them. He was quick to lump whites into an imagined privileged oppressor group against which he could organize his aggression and develop his adaptation; his only recourse, as he saw it, was an ethnic identification.

In addition to this repetitive ethnic focus, our voters associated their uncertain American identity with a perception of a declining work ethic. They felt the loss of a united society that included affordable education, safe schools, job security, community life, a manageable picture of crime and violence, recognizable national goals. Voters were deeply disaffected with politics and politicians, whom they felt were manipulative, dishonest, and driven by self-interest. They felt the judicial system was inefficient and overly litigious, with a jury system increasingly racially polarized and unsympathetic to ethnic Americans. Despite their shared anxiety, cynicism, alienation, and loss of faith in the system, voters were aware of their need to renegotiate their connections with others and with changing work environments in order to respond adequately to turbulence and change. They needed help to do this.

It seemed to me that these voters needed an interpretation, potentially offered by their leaders, which would both affirm and help them bear their painful experience by placing what they had repressed or dissociated in a larger context. This search for a larger context that allows both sides the possibility of hearing how the other is right is the primary challenge to the possibility of joining across differences as citizens.

Government leaders have the information and perspective to articulate the sources and social significance of rapid change, allowing voters to grasp their differentiated roles in an evolving society. Such an integrating interpretation, plus emotional containment and resources to connect with others, might have allowed voters to escape their experience as isolated individuals and find new ways to participate meaningfully in their world. They needed a synthesis of what they felt was the "partially" correct Republican picture (mobilized individual competence) in combination with the Democratic view (strength in diversity and community and resources for those in need). They grasped that individualism without community leads to deadening isolation and that unfettered welfare leads to over-dependence on the state. They needed help in figuring out how people could work together to learn from their differences and discover a larger frame of reference.

In order to engage the spectrum of voters, political leaders needed to recognize individual competence while affirming the importance of neighbors, neighborhood, and community. We felt in this study that leaders needed to articulate the dangers of isolation, acknowledge resource limitations (including their own), and define a mission that capitalized on American strength in diversity, a central value this country represented to the larger world. Leaders might have demonstrated how painful differences could be both affirmed and transcended in the service of an American identity. This would allow citizens to move beyond identifications with others in their subgroups toward an identity that both affirmed their individuality and allowed them to join a larger common purpose. The political polarization was interfering with hearing how the other side might be "right." Though the larger purpose required definition, what emerged in our study was the binding power of ethnicity and America's historical though periodically interrupted commitment to incorporating, recognizing, bridging, and transcending differences. This, it seemed, might be a recognizable American mission that citizens could have found a way to join.

The white majority and the election of 2000

These political trends in 1996 and the voters' wish for a synthesis contributed to the movement of both parties toward the middle. Despite significant differences in political philosophy, the election of 2000 showed little differences in the substance of the message from the two parties. Issues such as education, retirement security, and how to use economic prosperity captured the country's attention, but there was no significant effort to mobilize the competence of the electorate toward a larger vision, or to link America's internal national struggles to those of the outside world.

Just under the surface of these political discussions, the population was undergoing a significant change. Immigration, increasing ethnic identifications, and the emergence of major cultural voting blocks were changing the definition of "American." At the millennium, ethnic subgroups, once considered minorities, were becoming a larger part of the population, the majority in many cities and states. This change coincided with a similar shift away from the majority of American families being a heterosexual couple with their own biological children. The politics of diversity was moving into a new era.

When the results of the election of 2000 were finally made clear, it was obvious that an overwhelming number of minorities had been conveniently forgotten. In American society, whites have always held power and used it to increase the economic gap with non-whites. The white majority has managed a sense of unity through projection of difference. The unconscious message is, "We whites are all the same; you minorities are different." These dynamics, characteristic of unconscious group functioning, provided external support for ethnic bonding in racial and ethnic subgroups. As my interview with Frank illustrated, the shared (and understandable) feeling was, "If we ethnic minorities are not in power, at least we are unified."

In a country where disengaged and unintegrated citizens do not take up the complex work of democracy, the law increasingly regulates social and human issues. In 2000, the electoral process itself was handed over to the courts, de-linked from the democratic process and the Constitution. Perhaps in an unconscious recognition of the incipient loss of their majority, the white establishment seized power in a way that politicized the legal system and disenfranchised ethnic voters.

The turn

For a period of time after the 2000 election, it seemed as if the antipathy to the election process would contribute to a mediocre presidency and a dispirited American public. Despite post-election rhetoric about bringing people together across the political spectrum, there was evidence of familiar American conservative trends in the government's abandoning the ABM treaty for a National Missile Defense, withdrawing from collaborative international efforts around global warming, and providing tax relief for wealthy individuals. All three policies represented a retreat from joining a differentiated and integrated community and the substitution of an isolated, intensely defended individuality.

The terrorist attacks of September 11, 2001 transformed everything. Suddenly, the unconscious anxiety that non-whites would take the country over from within (manifest most clearly at the Republican center) was transformed into a shared conscious anxiety that non-whites (as "the other") would destroy America from without. From the perspective of the internal national split, the attack could be understood dynamically as a return of a dissociated mental representation of historical racism, causing massive psychic disruption and reorganization. The right-wing saw with shock its denied hatred of difference returning as an ethnic attack, the left saw its own disconnection from fundamental values returning as a rageful portrait of America's godless liberalism. The shock of recognition indicated that this defensively split construction of the national identity had not worked; it demanded an internal shift to acknowledge a more complex reality. Facing this transformation was a conservative Republican president and a management team experienced in war.

If America was struggling with a developmental internal split with fundamental values held internally and differences projected to the outer boundaries, the terrorist attack evoked a crisis. Americans—as revealed by our president—were stunned that outside ethnic groups hated them. They faced a manifest identity crisis between a narcissistic self-idealization (President

Bush called Americans "a good and kind people") and a vicious external retaliation for foreign policies that had contributed to the marginalization of ethnic subgroups.

Unlike the war in Vietnam, where the issues were complex and ambiguous and the dynamics suggested some form of American bullying, the war on terrorism offered clearly delineated "barbarians" who were ethnically identifiable. The recognition that "they are trying to kill us" mobilizes powerful defenses, and with a clearly recognized "all bad" external enemy, internal differences in the country momentarily disappeared in a moving surge of patriotism. But the developmental tension between experiencing all difference as outside versus discovering a sense of "otherness" within remained.

"Are we all 'Americans'—or just some of us?" This unresolved question was visible in the contrast between the moving obliteration of ethnic differences in the escape from the Twin Towers and the episodic vicious murder, beatings, and harassment of American Muslims and Sikhs across the country. Both of these responses are recognizable as historically American and as evidence of an unresolved struggle about American identity and values.

The Republican government's response to the attack was sophisticated, multilateral, and determined. The election promises of genuine delegation and decisiveness seemed fulfilled, as were the potentials for bipartisanship. And the media moved quickly into a massive educational forum about terrorism and a review of the motivations for such intense hatred of America. Citizens were beginning to learn about America's dynamic role in the world, the group projections onto the country, and the intense stereotyping that America has invited by its policies. Though America has contributed to international humanitarian aid, it has regularly supported oppressive regimes that act against its national values. These policies provided the basis for projective processes from abroad, supported by America's wealth, power, and relative isolation. Newscasts, managed and filtered by the white power elites, have maintained the country's isolation by focusing on local issues and paying scant attention to the larger world.

Terrified by its sudden vulnerability and after facing an unprovoked attack, America's response was to use its vast military might to attempt to destroy those disaffiliated ethnic groups that Americans experience as "other." As one general put it, "We must destroy the conditions that lead to terrorism." While the country had the power to be successful militarily, only coalition-building could support the deeper integration and renegotiation of identity that was needed. Without the coalition, the nation ran the risk of deepening its regressive narcissistic position of invulnerability that contributed to isolation, withdrawal, and mutual projection. This solution—enacted later in Donald Trump's "America First" position—entrenches the country in a familiarly rigid defensive posturing in which "otherness" remains projected out, its illusion of internal goodness and certainty is maintained, and the integration of internal differences is once more postponed.

America's sudden vulnerability, however, might also have been an opportunity to recognize the vulnerability of others and the need for Americans to help "ameliorate" rather than "destroy" the very conditions the nation had participated in developing. Recognizing internal ethnic tensions, Americans might have been more able to recognize their relatedness to the world's anger. This, sadly, did not happen.

We know about these dynamics. In my role as a therapist, for example, I have heard from some of my patients about their identification with the terrorists. I listen to their relentless hatred, envy, and wishes for retaliation and revenge against those with resources who withhold them in order to take care of themselves. When I worked with their families, I could see how this kind of polarization, rage, and marginalization could shift in treatment through identification with the "other" to an increasing recognition of guilt, concern, and connectedness. This shift from rage and paranoia to identification and grief is hard to come by in the absence of containment and interpretation.

Erik Erikson (1968) describes "integrity" as a commitment to the most mature meaning available, requiring the discovery of larger social tasks to which the individual can become committed (E. R. Shapiro & Fromm, 1999). After the attack in 2001, Americans had the opportunity to recognize their internal polarization and participate more fully in living out their values. Bush's retaliatory presidency did little to engage this opportunity.

Obama and Trump

The election of Barack Obama in 2008 mobilized an idealized fantasy of an America that could judge its citizens as Martin Luther King dreamed, "… not by the color of their skin but by the content of their character." Obama represented in his person the ultimate globalized ideal of integrating differences (black father, white mother, foreign upbringing). In the healing view that swept the country, many Americans discovered an identity that connected to their ideals and beliefs about the integration of difference—and America (transiently) deepened its ability to represent that identity to the world.

But underneath this phenomenon, the politics of isolation and the hatred of difference, so familiar in America's history, were intensifying. The frightening financial meltdown in 2007 had underscored the power of the coastal elites and illuminated Americans' perception of the corrupt (and, ultimately unpunished) exploitation of America's middle class. Despite Obama's competent management of the crisis, he increasingly came to represent to many from middle America both otherness and bi-coastal elitism. His support for marriage equality, respect for the gender spectrum, and willingness to stand up for liberal values became linked to the development of politically correct "trigger warnings" in colleges that protected the sensitivities of minorities and the traumatized and was perceived by conservatives as a limitation of their freedom of speech. The experience of middle America's voters in my 1996 interviews of feeling *"left out, voiceless or just numbers in a political game in which they simply did not count,"* grew and politicians ignored it. Affirmative action, protection of "otherness," even the Black Lives Matter movement had contributed to the underlying fantasy in the center of the country that, as whites were moving into the minority, their opportunities were disappearing.

In response, came Donald Trump. The black writer Ta-Nehisi Coates (2017) called Donald Trump "the first white president" noting in *Atlantic Magazine*, "Trump arrived in the wake of [what he and his base considered] … an entire nigger presidency with nigger healthcare, nigger climate accords, and nigger justice reform, all of which could be targeted for destruction or redemption, thus reifying the idea of being white." The Trump backlash was a familiar oscillation around America's identity challenge of integrating differences. Trump represented in his person the narcissistic isolation and repudiation of difference that has dogged America's history from its inception. His candidacy and his presidency mobilized ethnic hatred and racist behavior and was symbolized by the image of a wall that would exclude "the other." Like our waiter Frank, Trump could relate only to his narrow "base" considering others as "stupid," "rapists," and "enemies of the people." He could not take up membership, mature citizenship, or join the larger society and lead from that role. With his presidency, Americans were now looking at the worst representation of themselves and seeing clearly how difficult America's mission of integrating differences continues to be.

Individuals in authority roles have a large impact on people in organizations and society. To what extent does the personality of the leader have a major determining effect on the nature of the organization—or the state—and to what extent does the nature of the group, its tasks, structures, and relations with other groups influence the choice of its leaders? These questions have broad implications. If the group exists as an entity defined in relation to its task, then it, like the individual, is faced with the need to define itself in its context, that is, in relation to other groups. How, and why now, did America pick this particular leader? What is America saying to the rest of the world? What is the challenge now facing a disintegrating society?

Discussion

The dynamics of ethnicity, and minorities in general, have long been a major focus of irrational psychological and political behavior. Members of ethnic, and other, subgroups become symbols that hold emotional meaning; all diversity can serve as foci for projection. Black or Hispanic people in America, Aborigines in Australia, members of the LGBTQ community, disabled individuals—all of these minorities and anyone perceived as "different"—mobilize passionate political polarization (T. Singer, 1999). The easy unconscious use of differences as receptacles where feelings of inadequacy, vulnerability, threat, and damage can be located outside of the self, leads to social disintegration that becomes manifest in the fragmentation of families, the breakdown of nations, and the rise of fundamentalism, tribalism, and factionalism throughout society.

This polarity marks the understanding of irrational behavior in the behavior of individuals, groups, and nations. American identity was first crafted in opposition to experienced tyranny. The openness, spaciousness, and freedom in the nation supported a powerful sense of American individualism. As it developed, the country recognized the significance of community, of interdependence, in accomplishing national goals. Is America's current collective use and misuse of ethnic boundaries a larger-group manifestation of American individualism? Is the way its citizens so easily define themselves as individuals or in narrowly defined subgroups a collective defense against a difficulty in discerning a larger identity as Americans? Does America need an external enemy to discover the ways that freedom and interdependence are inseparable? Or, is it possible for Americans to finally discover a collective identity in which they learn from their differences, integrate their unique history and values, and face—without flinching—others' complex reactions to them?

There may be congruence between the way the white power elite currently see this nation and the way it is seen from the outside. The collective picture of America as a nation run by affluent, powerful white men, while manifestly accurate, is also a defensive compromise formation requiring a repression of its multiethnic complexity. Like any defensive structure, this view helps American citizens manage the anxiety derived from a full engagement with the nation's history and its internal diversity. Such a defensive American identity will inevitably continue to sap its citizens of the creative energy they might discover with a more complex integration of their differentiated strengths and capacities.

As Frank says, "If a black man represents the restaurant, the customers get scared." So long as this is true in America, the nation will not be able to sell convincingly its mission of integration, interdependence, and democracy to the world's customers. Though it is manifestly simpler to form identities along ethnic lines, Americans have psychological and political work to do in order to identify themselves with the nation's range of multiethnic citizens. And, if citizens discover that they cannot identify with some of those who are different, they might, in the service of the national mission, be able to approach those differences as opportunities for learning from diversity rather than to hate these others as "not us." At the moment, in 2019, this outcome still seems out of reach.

America, as a developing experiment in bringing together different ethnicities, histories, and capacities can have a significant international role in reducing the projective distinctions between the "good guys" and the "bad guys." This might reduce the dangers of political disintegration as ethnic conflicts challenge the integrity of existing multicultural nation states (Ferguson, 2001). In assuming its own mature responsibilities for contributing to the marginalization of subgroups both within and without, this country might offer a realistic hope for transcending differences in the service of a larger integrative mission. The hope for a more complex vision of a global community may depend in an evolving world on the integration of America's identity and its willingness to recognize that the so-called "good guys" have to take their share of responsibility for the creation of disorder and rage.

CHAPTER FOURTEEN

Citizenship as Development

To this point, I have suggested that an interpretive stance is possible through examining and negotiating experience with others across several roles within institutions. I've indicated how the role of the leader (CEO) requires attention to systems dynamics, the collaborative negotiation of a mission, and the mobilization of staff to make sense of their task-related experiences in role. I've now raised the possibility that nations, too, have missions that can contribute to the development of a global society. Thinking of nations along lines analogous with organizations, it is therefore possible to begin to discern the citizen role in a nation that is located in a global context. This is a grand idea indeed, but it is important not to lose sight of the psychological work individuals must undertake to find themselves within this matrix. That work is the focus of this chapter.

Mature adulthood inevitably involves membership in many groups. What is the developmental challenge we face in sorting out those multiple memberships and roles to approach the larger identity of citizen? In other words, how can we make sense of those connections between people and their groups that allow individuals to locate their own mature citizenship, that is, to recognize their connections to others, discover the authority for their unique perspective, and take the risk of speaking out?

Let's return to our two stories: Frank, the black waiter from Chicago, and Tom, the black British Anglican who stands up to the adolescents on the bus. When Frank says, "You are seen as black first. White males are hung up on power. If they can't control you, they diminish you," he is organizing his thinking around an ethnically visible enemy—white males—some of whom may have an equally stereotyped view of him. Frank lives in an American culture where the history of slavery has led to pervasive political and social pressures that contribute to ethnic stereotyping. His psychological adaptation to these pressures is to join this simplified picture of society. This allows him to explain his problems in life: He blames white men, a group to which he does not and cannot belong, for his limitations. Discovering such a clearly delineated enemy (the "other") leads to the notion that if only "they" would disappear, life would be easier. A recognizable external enemy to blame limits the possibility of noticing, learning from, and mastering a more complex world (Erlich, 1997; E. R. Shapiro, 2004). Looking outside of the self inhibits the potential for facing internal limitations and engaging the world more fully.

Having focused his aggression outside of himself, Frank cannot locate his capacity for citizenship, nor recognize it in others. "No one is in charge," he says. "It is just happening." He feels as though he has no voice in the world and is hopeless about ever being in charge of his life. Joining a polarized subgroup in the mind can be a first developmental step—and an adaptive choice—to emerge from social isolation. It can solve an experience of unbearable aloneness and impotence. But taking up membership in the larger society takes further internal work.

Tom is in a different place internally—and he has the advantage of coming from a British political culture, where the history of colonialization and the development of a Commonwealth has created a more complex social response to difference. Watching black adolescents causing trouble for a white bus driver at a time of social unrest, Tom notes that, "None of the white passengers moved or intervened in any way," and says to himself, with some irritation and anxiety, "Why do I have to do this?" before telling the kids to contain themselves. Tom finds a different solution from Frank. He moves from seeing potential danger to initially feeling lost and alone. First, like Frank, he locates himself within a recognizable group—in this case, a group based on colour (Tom says, "None of the white passengers moved or intervened in any way"). However, Tom then takes up leadership, intervenes, and succeeds, raising in the process his central question, "Why do *I* have to do this?"

Tom's story is unremarkable: Such conflicts occur daily; not all of us take up the challenge when we see it. But when Tom does, his decision is almost forced on him by a complex set of internal and external pressures—influenced by the varied set of roles and groups to which he belongs. Though we know little about Tom's institutional roles and tasks, we know about his other memberships. These include his being a social worker, embedded in a disciplinary organization with a mission focused on those at the lower end of society; his ethnic identity as black, with instinctive sympathy and empathy toward with this group; his religious commitment, mobilized in terms of caring for the passengers, the driver, and the young people; his experience and role as a father; and his identification as a British citizen. The story raises many questions. Who says Tom "has to" act? Are the pressures he experiences coming from his personal psychology or from the social surround? What internalized group is he joining, why, and through what process? And, for whom is he responding?

At the end of his story, Tom adds that he did not like the role he was in. Does he mean that this citizenship role does not feel like a part of him? How can such a thing happen? And how does Tom's taking leadership in this instance help clarify Frank's paralysis? Can we even consider these matters without recognizing the different political and social cultures from which these two men come?

We are focusing on the developmental transition from an isolated individual like Frank—filled with anger and blame—to an actively functioning member of society like Tom, who can take on the role of leader in the service of a larger community. These two stories—picked out of different cultures—illuminate the ways we are all immersed in the multiple subgroupings of our larger society; they underline the work necessary to make the transition to fully joining society. To move beyond the individual, we must return to the group.

Roles and groups

Throughout our development we gain membership in an increasing number of groups. First with the family, then with our peers as children, and, finally, with adulthood, social pressure comes from the much larger human contexts in which we live. To take full charge of our own lives and find a place to stand as a citizen requires an effort to make sense of these connections and their impact on us. This begins with our engagement in organizations. Taking up a role in an organization connects each of us with *mission*: the links—both explicit and hidden—that each organization must make to the needs of the larger society. Through our organizational *roles*—the place where the person and the context meet—we can begin to have a public voice on behalf of others.

But as we enter the larger society, we meet powerful irrational pressures. Society is an unstructured large group composed of familiar subgroupings (nations, ethnic groups, religions, social groups, organizations), but being able to name these components does not make the world more transparent; society—as a whole—is too large and remains ungraspable. Nonetheless, once we notice that social pressures impinge on us, we cannot ignore them. So, we attempt to organize our experience—both internally and externally—in order to maintain a reasonably stable sense of ourselves. We do this in two ways: personally, and politically. The personal is the development of a psychological "skin" so as to relate to others while holding onto oneself. This skin is a textured boundary that allows us a space to assess the impact of others and consider our reactions to them. The political is the attempt to simplify the world by *imagining oneself in some kind of group* that links to and involves others.

This process begins by making reciprocal relationships with others. But, as an individual becomes more aware of his needs, if he is unable to negotiate relationships with larger numbers of people, he can protect himself by using projection. Through this mechanism, he locates the undesirable parts of himself in others and blames others for those parts. By doing so, it is possible to perceive those people as separate. If "they" are white, *I* can locate myself in a discernible subgroup—*in my mind*—which provides a kind of membership, and "we" are black. This is Frank's position.

Joining such a group requires me to let go, at least momentarily, of some of my complexity as an individual. In order to merge in my mind with other members of my chosen group, I must surrender something. This blurring of distinctions in order to join is called *regression*. In popular use, this term carries pejorative overtones. But the notion, in fact, is value neutral and describes the way we can return from one process, one way of thinking, to a developmentally earlier one. The most familiar form of regression is from autonomy into a dependent mode, from "I can manage by myself" to "I need them." This dependent regression can make me less threatening to the group, since I am trying to find common cause in order to belong.

As we define ourselves and organize our internal worlds by polarizing ourselves into a group in relation to "the others" (as Frank did), we can begin to focus and make some sense of the anxiety, aggression, alienation, and other unmanageable feelings that derive from the chaos of living in today's world. Without some kind of group that begins to articulate a collective way of viewing the world, the world can seem incomprehensible. And this effort is not just private. The fact that we see ourselves as members of a particular subgroup alters our relationships with the other members.

Frank found a way to manage his anger about his professional limitations by using projection. He locates both his ambitions and his devaluation in a white-male outside group. This way, he creates a relatively secure but inflexible environment which he cannot test against a larger reality. To become a participating mature citizen, he would have to increase his flexibility, reduce his biases, and open the possibility of joining something larger. Frank's thinking contributes to his lack of hope and is also exacerbated by the behaviour of some white people in America, who collude with his projections by behaving prejudicially towards him and other African Americans.

As such, Frank cannot fully experience himself as an individual American struggling with diverse opportunities and complex constraints. Instead, he locates himself almost exclusively as a "black man." He polarizes his internal groups, locating "the others" in the white world. *His* group in his mind—holding his primary experience—is shaped by the imagined context of other African Americans who, he believes, passionately and deeply share his picture of the ethnically oriented social world around them. Frank lumps white people into an imagined privileged oppressor group against which he can organize his aggression and develop his adaptation.

This is a constricted adult role, but it can be mobilized politically. Closely held group identity and shared traditions can allow for the development of a political position and a political voice. If I am a black man and understand the history, trauma, and current conditions of black people in America, I can articulate these issues, check with my group about how accurately I understand them, and stand up in public with the possibility that I am representing them. If I am successful, I am a representative of a group and I have a voice. But can I lead others outside my group from that role? (This is the position of Donald Trump, who could not find a way beyond his constricted identification with his "base" to represent and lead the larger American society.)

Frank is too committed to himself and his subgroup. Frank says, "My business is to take care of me"—but at whose expense? He says, "The customers get scared," but of what? Though Frank may vote, he votes as an isolate or, at best, as a member of a subgroup, but not as a member of the wider community. The social–psychological place he represents as an individual is disconnected from the respectful negotiation necessary to engage and build a citizenry. But Frank's experience does represent a potential political voice, with passionately held information from a defined community that the larger society needs to listen to in order to build a more comprehensive integration. To be a more widely engaged citizen, Frank would have to pull back his hatred and recognize that his customers *are* related to him; they are fellow citizens. In a racist America, this is not easy to accomplish. Citizenship, however, is not a personal attribute, not just a political stance, and not just a vote—it is a corporate concept that includes joining the diversities of a nation (Khaleelee, 1994).

Of course, the nation, too, has its responsibilities. Frank, like so many others, is influenced by projective processes within society. Subgroups that carry messages, stories, and meanings that are difficult for society to face and integrate—ethnic minorities, LGBTQ, psychiatric patients, the physically impaired, traumatized veterans, and others—are often marginalized in order "to silence the messenger" (Elmendorf & Parish, 2007). As a consequence of society's pressures and his own development, Frank is stuck; he does not experience his vote as a symbol of freedom and full recognition of his membership in society. For Frank, his vote is a weapon against an oppressive society not an opportunity to join it fully. To join others—and be joined by them—requires a creative search for linking contexts.

Tom, on the other hand, has made these connections. As the dispute on the bus unfolds, Tom initially relates to the group of ethnic black teenagers in his mind; he knows well his place in the black and West Indian subculture of suburban London. The resulting role of black male adult allows him to grasp the anger and rebellious acting out of the black adolescents, moving him toward an empathic identification with them against the (white) authority of the bus driver. Tom's initial polarization is not unlike that of Frank. But we all belong to many groups, some consciously and some out of our awareness. These multiple memberships are aspects of identity—and elements of our functioning as citizens. Unlike Frank, Tom remembers his other groups. For example, he may have also identified with British culture (through his membership of the Church of England or elsewhere) and the transient social threat of feeling unprotected during the firemen's strike. Holding this role would inevitably precipitate a conflict for him with his role as a black man. Managing the tension inside himself might have shifted Tom into feeling that only he, in the bus, could face the adolescents' aggression and help them recognize the social consequences of acting it out.

Tom was faced with a crisis: danger was happening, and he knew something about it. He had to decide who he was in order to locate himself. His report indicates his awareness of many of his internalized groups and his effort to integrate them without diminishing any. He had to discover the connections between his multiple memberships by discovering a larger context, one in which both the teenagers and the larger society could be "right"—not morally (since harassing bus drivers is wrong), but understandably. Uncovering *how* "the other" is right is the first step in our interpretive stance that is aimed at discovering the connections that lead to shared membership.

In their presumed misunderstanding of each other, both the driver and the youths were locked into a drama that, if acted out, might have physically injured those who were directly involved and ultimately damaged race relations. But Tom was able to offer the adolescents the possibility of identifying with his integration of roles—black adult male, church member, father, and citizen—so they could place their reactions in perspective.

We can now begin to answer some of the questions Tom raises. First, he asks, "Why do *I* have to do this?" This is a question each citizen must face. Taking up a citizen role requires work—and social engagement includes risk. "Why me?" signals a recognition that "I am at stake here"—and is a protest against the risk. What forces would make any individual risk himself on behalf of others? What allows any individual to identify with the whole group so that he knows if they are at risk, he is as well?

Tom makes the transition from a member of a subgroup to a citizen. To grasp this transition requires us to review Tom's roles and the social task each entails. The first is his role as a black adult male. Tom can feel the anger of the black youths without being too afraid of it; he is one of them, and he sees how their anger is "right." He can convey this to the young people without endorsing their current behavior. Second, through his role as a church member, he has identified with the transcendent interdependency that belief in God entails. Feeling part of a social whole, Tom can experience the vulnerability of the larger society. Finally, in his family role as father, Tom can respond to the adolescents' developmental need for a limiting context—a paternal presence—at the moment of their rebellion against authority.

Tom also says, "I don't like this role." His unhappiness points to his role conflict. Identified as a black man, Tom would inevitably be irritated at the adolescents' disturbance, which casts an unfavorable image of black males. Nonetheless, understanding their anger, he might also unconsciously be tempted to side with them. But though he brought some of his resentment into his decision to act—thinking, "Why do I, a black man, have to take up a leadership role in a society that treats black people badly?"—Tom ultimately overcame the temptation to devalue the rest of his roles.

If he had the space to reflect on this process, he might have recognized that in his role conflict he was containing—and potentially unconsciously solving—a significant social tension between his ethnic identity and his larger sense of British citizenship. This kind of resolution—if unpacked—might inform us about the components of social impasse and some of the linking ideas that allow for joining the larger society. Tom's resolution—to ask the kids to be respectful—represented both this internal solution and his good-enough integration of these multiple roles. This may account for the quality of his insight to the youths, offering the strike of the firefighters as a shared context within which aggression must be contained.

In the light of all this, Tom's question, "Why me? Why do *I* have to do this?" can be seen as a question about his integrity. To be all of himself requires him to face his connections to others and the values embedded in these memberships. His question might be translated as: "What groups am I in now and in what roles? And, how do I bridge them—and join this society as a citizen?"

These are dilemmas for all of us. When engaged in tension-filled dialogue, the temptation is to treat "the others" disrespectfully by assigning them to a devalued role and dismissing them (as Frank does). Considering people as "others" has always been an easy solution to social conflict. We do this by unconsciously choosing an exclusive subgroup to which to belong. This allows us to deny the ways in which, by disconnecting the others, we are also alienating parts of ourselves that we cannot stand.

Choosing a polarized group is only the first step. As Tom did, we can also discover groups that *bridge* differences. We are each embedded in more groups than we realize or ever know. Their tasks and meanings are in our minds, if we search for them. Facing conflict with another person, we might be able to allow ourselves to wonder which groups—in our minds—might link the differing perspectives we are hearing and feeling. And we might consider negotiating a shared membership with others in order to discover a way out of disconnection and impasse. In the tense conflict between the driver and the youths, for instance, Tom interposed their shared membership as British citizens. This larger context constitutes a third party to the two groups that are in apparent opposition. If perceived as a structured group, it both contains and defines the pair within a task and set of values that can be used to help contain and connect the apparent conflict. This solution is often used in efforts to mediate conflict. For example, American presidents' repeated efforts to bring Palestinians and Israelis together have regularly used their shared membership in a larger context as "people of the Book" to facilitate dialogue.

There are, of course, limitations to this method of exploration. In our story, Tom said, "Back off," to the adolescents at some personal risk. He set a limit to their aggression—containment as a precondition for exploration and discovery.

Discovering a bridging group is both a creative effort and an example of leadership. We often unconsciously negotiate such "institutions-in-the-mind" in order to manage in a controlled way our inevitable regressions in the face of the threatening power that our complex society represents. Roles within institutions—related to institutional tasks—begin to enable us to establish sufficient self-definition to examine and then competently assume the necessary larger range of social roles within society. Tom's internal work allowed him, however reluctantly, to take up fully and with integrity the effective leadership role and identity of "participating citizen."

These notions—joining, membership, mission, containment, and roles—represent some of the steps an individual takes toward social interpretation from within the self. Integration of these roles into a coherent identity allows identification with the larger social context and the beginnings of membership. But being able to join the world as member is different from taking up a role as citizen-leader. That role must be negotiated with others. Though we can use our memberships, roles, and task contexts to begin to speak to one another, there might be additional ways to study these social interactions and the organizational and institutional contexts that help create them in order to better grasp how our society is functioning. I will explore this possibility further in Chapter Fifteen.

CHAPTER FIFTEEN

Society as a Multicellular Learning System

We begin as members of our families and learn our family roles as the family engages in its developmental task. We take our transgenerational family histories and our family role perspectives into our groups and organizations. Through those aspects of identity, we begin to make sense of our outside world; they inform our participation as citizens. If our institutional leaders authorize an interpretive stance for their staff that supports taking seriously one's own experience in role and that of others, we can begin to develop self-reflective institutions. Using our institutional missions as lenses onto the outer world, we can engage other institutions with related missions to broaden our understanding of society. Though our missions will inevitably be challenged by internal and external pressures and we will periodically get lost, we can regain our task focus with outside help when needed. Our institutions, religions, nations, and other organized groups all have task links to the larger society. Each of us has the potential of integrating our experience in our multiple group and organizational roles toward a coherent sense of ourselves as citizens.

Given these considerations, it is perhaps possible to conceive of humanity as a multicellular learning system, with each of us as a working cell. Such a system would learn by forming bounded entities of multiple cells (groups, institutions, religions, nations). Each entity would be configured by the emerging coherence of individual motivations and histories as well as the shaping of an institutional identity through engagement with the outside world. Each entity would have missions that take up particular aspects of learning on behalf of the whole. Taking this perspective might allow us to begin to recognize and articulate the different ways we are working at social learning in our various bounded entities. Consolidation of learning and the integrative development of the human system would then take place across the boundaries of working groups.

This is an optimistic, and possibly idealistic, perspective organized around the possibility that human development is a collectively unconscious drive that motivates and impacts our social functioning. There is another side. Society can also develop a set of defenses that can hold an otherwise diverse community together but may interfere with social learning and development.

For example, Volkan (1998, 2006a, 2006b) describes powerful forces—*chosen glories* and *chosen trauma*—that can mobilize large populations to consolidate their identities. These are mental representations of significant historical events shared by all members of the group and contributing to their collective identity. These images can support the group and bring members together at times of collective stress.

Chosen glories are idealized myths or historical triumphs marked by pride and pleasure that are passed down from generation to generation, recollected ritualistically, and serving as markers of a large group's identity. Reactivation of chosen glories brings people together and increases the population's self-esteem without evoking hostility toward others. Thanksgiving in America is an example of such a chosen glory, mythologizing a history that might otherwise have been seen as a rapacious conquering of a poorly defended native population. This example makes evident how one group's chosen glory can be another group's chosen trauma.

Chosen traumas are shared mental representations, sometimes unconscious but potentially available, of events in a large group's history where the group has suffered catastrophic loss, humiliation, and helplessness at the hands of its enemies. When chosen traumas are reactivated, sometimes by political leaders, they can stimulate a large population of otherwise diverse people to uncover a shared identity, re-evoking feelings of humiliation and driving wishes for revenge against the other.

Volkan (2006b) says:

> When members of a victim group are unable to mourn such losses and reverse their humiliation and helplessness, they pass on to their

offspring the images of their injured selves and psychological tasks that need to be completed. This process is known as the "transgenerational transmission of trauma." All such images contain references to the same historical event. As decades pass, the mental representation of this event links all the individuals in the large group and emerges as a significant large group identity marker. Such reactivation can be used by political leaders to initiate and fuel entitlement ideologies and promote new massive societal movements, some of them malignant.

In the context of this book's argument about human development, an otherwise diverse population forming itself around such chosen trauma might be understood as a regressive phenomenon. Such a regression might be evoked by the failure of more task-focused entities to clarify and link their missions to the ideals, beliefs, and needs of the developing larger society.

Humanity has made a number of efforts at intergroup learning (Soviet Union, United Nations, European Union). Their success as learning enterprises depended on their capacity to link their consolidated learning to meaningful missions. For example, the European Union was formed around sophisticated economic thinking. Efforts to bring together a common market and a common trading block made a great deal of practical sense. The agenda, largely concealed from the populace and without their informed permission, was political union without political accountability. The EU failed to take fully into account the conflicting and passionately held national identities and missions of its members. Though the various EU management structures were representative, irrational outbursts between members of historically warring nations regularly broke out in otherwise rational economic discussions. One of the consequences of the larger entity's political disconnection from citizens of member nations is that many have experienced the "EU-in-the-mind" as an impersonal and powerful "Brussels." The UK in particular demonstrates this with the narrowly won vote in 2016 to leave the EU, and the resulting chaos of Brexit—and nationalistic impulses are breaking out all across Europe. The anxiety about the loss of national identity seems to have made it difficult to understand and learn from the promise of coming together.

The ideas I am presenting here are difficult. Considering them requires adopting the listening position that runs through this book: How is the other right? Such a position inevitably undercuts the projective use of others as "not me," a defense which, with difficulty, we might consider relaxing in relation to certain other people—but would be much more difficult in response to enemy nations. Using this framework, however, the role of global citizen might begin to have definition, beginning with institutional membership, an authorized representative function, and the possibility of cross-entity interpretation. From this perspective, one function of leadership is to recognize the interdependence of institutional missions in relation to the overarching task of societal development. With support for the development of an internal interpretive stance and the resultant capacity to develop institutional representatives to engage an external interpretive function with other institutions, we might develop consolidated cross-institutional structures that stand for social learning (see Chapter Thirteen).

If humanity survives the current nationalistic regression and fragmentation and faces the existential threats of global warming, nuclear proliferation, environmental degradation, and overpopulation, some recognition of the need for an increasingly integrated world will persist. This will ultimately require coherent political processes leading toward a functioning political leadership system. To date, this has been difficult to accomplish. One of the difficulties has been our struggle to find appropriately bounded larger contexts that can integrate differing perspectives toward shared meaning. This has contributed to our failure to adopt a shared interpretive methodology that takes seriously experiences in roles within institutions and within nations, and to develop leadership that can authorize the learning task on behalf of the whole.

In a speech to the economic gathering at Davos, the director of programming, Sebastian Buckup (2019) noted:

> The current global architecture was shaped by the Great Depression and two devastating World Wars—and it certainly did shape us in return. It gave birth to a world that has little in common with the one by which it was created: China, which in the 1940s was an isolated, agrarian country torn apart by civil war, is now a leading global power in everything from artificial intelligence to wireless technologies; the European Union, which was meant to create an "ever closer union" in Europe is fracturing from within; and the United States, which for most of the postwar era was the dominant driver of globalization, is now neglecting or even leaving some of the multilateral institutions it championed.

In this new world, global cooperation is on the defense, and the architecture we built to sustain globalization is eroding. But a new era of globalization is nevertheless knocking on the world's door, with digital trade, online IP rights, cyber attacks, and the problems posed by climate change becoming ever more relevant.

Humanity is not short of big ideas, nor does it lack powerful tools. What it does lack is an architecture for these to scale up for the greater good. We have no blueprint for such an architecture, but the technology that challenges the old is likely to be at its core. Cities and states won't disappear, but digital tools will assume many of their mandates … New powers, problems, and technological possibilities are pushing hard against structures that were built for other purposes and other times. We need a new architecture—but where to start?

It might be that if the interpretive capacity I've attempted to explore in this book could be recognized and engaged, we could develop such a "new architecture," inevitably internet linked but more connected to the needs of the larger society. Those of us who are willing to engage in this process might then find ways, as Tom did, to integrate the values and beliefs that lie behind our various memberships. We might, then, through our institutional roles, begin to make some collective sense of our world. These would be steps toward global citizenship.

Conclusion

I began this exploration by underlining the ways we are inextricably embedded in our social context. The psychoanalyst, Donald Winnicott (1960), famously noted that "there is no such thing as a baby," recognizing that it is the mother–baby pair that defines the individual from the very beginning. Though we begin to develop a sense of ourselves as separate individuals from within the family group and sharpen that recognition throughout adulthood, the impact on us of the social context never goes away. Whether we pay attention to it or not, we are all delegates of our families, representatives of our multigenerational, cultural, ethnic, and gender histories, and members of our institutions. The question I've attempted to address in this book is whether we can make that representative function more conscious so that we can use it to deepen our participation in our ever-more rapidly changing society.

What does it mean to be a member of society? Humankind is moving in the direction of greater awareness of the collective. Though global warming and internet technology are underlining our necessary interdependence, the social power of what I have called our *bounded entities* is an underutilized resource. We begin life as members of a family; there is a further developmental sequence of joining that involves taking the risk of listening to how the other might be right and discovering larger contexts that connect us across differences. However, for any one of us to see himself as a member of humanity with a representative voice is a leap beyond the capacity of any individual. We need to use our institutional perspectives together to find our way in.

I have attempted to illustrate that an untapped power of our various bounded entities, our institutions, is that they provide access points to society. We have lenses onto the larger world through our institutional roles in ways that might make a difference if we learned how to use them collectively. My effort in this book has been to increase our awareness of that possibility.

I began by outlining the steps toward joining: listening for how the other is right, containing intense feelings so that there is a space for learning, taking seriously our experience in our roles, and negotiating interpretations with others. I laid out a number of challenges for institutional leaders: focusing on systems psychodynamics, sharpening the links between mission and the needs of society, authorizing an interpretive stance, and developing self-reflective institutions. And, finally, I've raised the possibility of cross-institutional interpretation as a way to make better sense of aspects of our larger social context.

One notion deserves a final bit of focused attention. While taking our experiences seriously, listening for how the other might be right, and negotiating shared interpretations will not come easily, for any individual to respond to interpersonal dialogue though his or her identification in role (as an aspect of an institutional mission) will be even more difficult. Exercising this discipline will inevitably challenge our belief that we are separate individuals and expose our vulnerability to have our feelings hurt.

As I discussed in Chapter Four, we will need institutional support to distinguish between our personal *relationships* with other people and our *relatedness* through our roles to the institution's mission. For example, if the young psychologist trainee in Chapter Three tells her older male supervisor that his putting his feet on the children's chairs makes her uncomfortable, what kind of institutional culture will help him to contain his inevitable defensiveness and consider that his actions might reflect something about his organization? When the new CEO in Chapter Nine tries to sit at the head of the table at lunch and is abruptly told by his staff that he can't sit there, what does it take for him to manage his inevitable reaction to what looks like a challenge to his authority so that he can listen and learn what the organization is trying to teach him? We will need to develop institutional cultures that contain our inevitable narcissistic injuries, support our capacities to bring ourselves fully into our roles, and help us to shape and identify with our institutional missions.

But the transformative possibilities are myriad. For example, workers in an airplane factory might see their jobs as making parts for airplanes. In a more self-reflective institution with a more sharply defined mission, they might experience their work as helping the nation to defend itself. Such an altered experience gives a social perspective, a transcendent reference, allowing workers to link their values and beliefs and their work experience to the needs of the larger society.

Though formal authorization as a citizen comes with birth or naturalization, effective citizenship is an interdependent experience. The capacity to link personal experience in role in relation to a task—with the support of increasingly socially linked, self-reflective institutions and leaders—may ultimately increase the possibility for each of us to find a place to stand.

References

Armstrong, D. (2006). *Organization in the Mind*. London: Routledge.
Barber, B. (1995). *Jihad vs. McWorld: Terrorism's Challenge to Democracy*. New York: Ballantine.
Bass, B. M. (1990). *Handbook of Leadership*. New York: Free Press.
Bennis, W. (1989). *Why Leaders Can't Lead: The Unconscious Conspiracy Continues*. San Francisco, CA: Jossey-Bass.
Berkowitz, D. A., Shapiro, R. L., Zinner, J., & Shapiro, E. R. (1974a). Family contributions to narcissistic disturbances in adolescents. *International Review of Psycho-Analysis, 1*: 353–362.
Berkowitz, D. A., Zinner, J., Shapiro, R. L., & Shapiro, E. R. (1974b). Concurrent family treatment of narcissistic disorders in adolescence. *International Journal of Psychoanalytic Psychotherapy, 3*(4): 379–396.
Bion, W. R. (1961). *Experiences in Groups and Other Papers*. London: Tavistock.
Bion, W. R. (1977). Attention and interpretation: container and contained. In: *Seven Servants: Four Works*. New York: Jason Aronson.
Buckup, S. (2019). Shaping global architecture in an era of fortresses and walls. [Presentation.] World Economic Forum, Davos, January 21.
Carr, A. W. (1985). *The Priestlike Task*. London: SPCK.
Carr, A. W. (1993). Some consequences of conceiving society as a large group. *Group: Journal of the Eastern Group Psychotherapy Society, 17*: 235–244.

Carr, A. W., & Shapiro, E. R. (1989). What is a "Tavistock" interpretation? In: A. W. Carr & F. Gabelnick (Eds.), *Proceedings of the International Symposium* (pp. 53–58). Washington, DC: A. K. Rice Institute.

Center for National Policy (1996). *Diagnosing Voter Discontent*. Washington, DC: CNP.

Coates, T. (2017). The first White President. *Atlantic Magazine*, October.

Elmendorf, D., & Parish, M. (2007). Silencing the messenger: The social dynamics of treatment resistance. *Journal of the American Academy of Psychoanalysis and Dynamic Psychiatry, 35*(3): 375–392.

Erikson, E. H. (1950). *Childhood and Society*. New York: W. W. Norton.

Erikson, E. H. (1956). The problem of ego identity. *Journal of the American Psychoanalytic Association, 4*: 56–121.

Erikson, E. H. (1958a). The nature of clinical evidence. *Daedalus: Journal of the American Academy of Arts and Sciences, 87*(4): 65–87.

Erikson, E. H. (1958b). *Young Man Luther: A Study in Psychoanalysis and History*. New York: W. W. Norton.

Erikson, E. H. (1968). *Identity, Youth and Crisis*. New York: W. W. Norton.

Erlich, S. (1997). On discourse with an enemy. In: E. R. Shapiro (Ed.), *The Inner World in the Outer World*. New York: Yale University Press.

Ferguson, N. (2001, December 2). 2011. *New York Times Magazine*.

Fraher, A. L. (2004). *A History of Group Study and Psychodynamic Organizations*. London: Free Association.

Fromm, M. G. (2006). A view from Riggs: Treatment resistance and patient authority–II. Transmission of trauma and treatment resistance. *Journal of the American Academy of Psychoanalysis and Dynamic Psychiatry, 34*: 445–458.

Fromm, M. G. (2007). The escalating use of medications by college students: What are they telling us, what are we telling them? *Journal of College Student Psychotherapy, 21*(3/4): 27–44.

Fromm, M. G. (Ed.) (2011). *Lost in Transmission: Studies of Trauma Across Generations*. New York: Karnac.

Gould, L., Stapley, L., & Stein, M. (2006). *The Systems Psychodynamics of Organizations: Integrating the Group Relations Approach, Psychoanalytic and Open Systems Perspectives*. New York: Routledge.

Harvard Business Review (1992). Boston, MA: Harvard Business School.

Havens, L. (1976). *Participant Observation*. New York: Jason Aronson.

Heifetz, R. A. (1994). *Leadership without Easy Answers*. Cambridge: Harvard University Press.

Heifetz, R. A., & Laurie, D. (1997). The work of leadership. *Harvard Business Review*, January: 124–134.

Hendry, J., & Johnson, G. (Eds.) (1993). *Strategic Thinking, Leadership and the Management of Change*. Chichester, UK: John Wiley.

Hirschhorn, L. (1988). *The Workplace Within*. Cambridge: MIT Press.

Hirschhorn, L. (1990). Leaders and followers in a post-industrial age: A psychodynamic view. *Journal of Applied Behavioral Science, 26*: 529–542.

Hirschhorn, L., & Gilmore, T. (1993). The boundaries of the "boundaryless" company. In: R. Howard & R. D. Haas (Eds.), *The Learning Imperative: Managing People for Continuous Innovation*. Cambridge, MA: Harvard Business School Press.

Jaques, E. (1955). Social systems as a defense against persecutory and depressive anxiety. In: G. Gabbard, J. Hartman, & R. Mann (Eds.), *Analysis of Groups*. San Francisco, CA: Jossey-Bass, 1974.

Jewson, D. (1997). Personal communication.

Kanter, R. M. (1989). *When Giants Learn to Dance: Mastering the Challenges of Strategy, Management and Careers in the 1990s*. New York: Simon & Schuster.

Kelly, J. (1993). *Facts against Fictions of Executive Behavior: A Critical Analysis of What Managers Do*. Westport, CT: Quorum.

Kernberg, O. (1966). Structural derivatives of object relationships. *International Journal of Psycho-Analysis, 47*: 236–253.

Kernberg, O. (1975). *Borderline Conditions and Pathological Narcissism*. New York: Jason Aronson.

Kernberg, O. (1976). *Object-Relations Theory and Clinical Psychoanalysis*. New York: Jason Aronson.

Kernberg, O. (1998). *Ideology, Conflict, and Leadership in Groups and Organizations*. New Haven, CT: Yale University Press.

Khaleelee, O. (1994). New futures: New citizenship. In: R. Bout, J. Lawrence, & J. Morris (Eds.), *Managing the Unknown, by Creating New Futures*. London: McGraw-Hill.

Khaleelee, O., & Miller, E. J. (1985). Beyond the small group: Society as an intelligible field of study. In: M. Pines (Ed.), *Bion and Group Psychotherapy*. London: Routledge & Kegan Paul.

Klein, E. B., Gabelnick, F., & Herr, P. (Eds.) (1998). *The Psychodynamics of Leadership*. Madison, CT: Psychosocial Press.

Klein, M. (1946). Notes on some schizoid mechanisms. *International Journal of Psycho-Analysis*, 27: 99–110.

Krantz, J. (1990). Lessons from the field: An essay on the crisis of leadership in contemporary organizations. *Journal of Applied Behavioral Science, 26*: 49–64.

Krantz, J. (1998). Anxiety and the new order. In: E. B. Klein, F. Gabelnick, & P. Herr (Eds.), *The Psychodynamics of Leadership*. Madison, CT: Psychosocial Press.

Lawrence, G. (1998). Unconscious social pressures on leaders. In: E. B. Klein, F. Gabelnick, & P. Herr (Eds.), *The Psychodynamics of Leadership*. Madison, CT: Psychosocial Press.

Lofgren, D. P. (1991). The temporary failure of an organization to move beyond charismatic leadership. Presentation at the Tenth Scientific Meeting of the A. K. Rice Institute (unpublished).

Lofgren, D. P. (1992). A developmental model of charisma and charismatic leadership: An examination of charisma from a psychoanalytic/group and object relations perspective. Presentation at McLean Hospital Academic Conference (unpublished).

Menzies, I. E. P. (1960). A case-study in the functioning of social systems as a defense against anxiety. *Human Relations, 13*: 95–121.

Miller, E. J. (Ed.) (1976). *Task and Organization*. London: Wiley.

Miller, E. J. (1989). The "Leicester" model: Experiential study of group and organizational processes. *Tavistock Institute of Human Relations Occasional Paper No. 10*. London: Tavistock.

Miller, E. J. (1998). The leader with the vision. In: E. B. Klein, F. Gabelnick, & P. Herr (Eds.), *The Psychodynamics of Leadership*. Madison, CT: Psychosocial Press.

Miller, E. J., & Rice, A. K. (1967). *Systems of Organization: The Control of Task and Sentient Boundaries*. London: Tavistock.

Miller, E. J., & Stein, M. (1993). Individual and organization in the 1990s: Time for a rethink? *The Tavistock Institute Review*, 35–37.

Mintz, D. (2002). Meaning and medication in the care of treatment resistant patients. *American Journal of Psychotherapy, 56*(3): 322–337.

Modell, A. H. (1975). A narcissistic defense against affects and the illusion of self-sufficiency. *International Journal of Psycho-Analysis, 56*: 275–282.

Modell, A. H. (1976). The "holding environment" and the therapeutic action of psychoanalysis. *Journal of the American Psychoanalytic Association, 24*: 285–307.

Modell, A. H. (1984). *Psychoanalysis in a New Context*. New York: International Universities Press.

Muller, J. P., & Tillman, J. G. (Eds.) (2007). *The Embodied Subject: Minding the Body in Psychoanalysis*. New York: Jason Aronson.

Obholzer, A., & Roberts, V. Z. (Eds.) (1994). *The Unconscious at Work*. London: Routledge.

Palmer, B. (1979). Learning and the group experience. In: W. G. Lawrence (Ed.), *Exploring Individual and Organisational Boundaries* (pp. 169–192). London: Wiley.

Parish, M. (2007). Reflections on the administrator's role. *Organisational and Social Dynamics, 7*(1): 61–72.

Pelton, W. J., Sackmann, S., & Boguslaw, R. (1990). *Tough Choices: The Decision-Making Styles of America's Top 50 CEOs*. Homewood, IL: Dow Jones-Irwin.

Perry, C. J., Fowler, J. C., Bailey, A., Clemence, A. J., Plakun, E. M., Zheutlin, B., & Speanburg, S. (2009). Improvement and recovery from suicidal and self-destructive phenomena in treatment-refractory disorders. *Journal of Nervous and Mental Disease, 197*(1): 28–34.

Plakun, E. M. (Ed.) (2011). *Treatment Resistance and Patient Authority: The Austen Riggs Reader*. New York: W. W. Norton.

Rice, A. K. (1966). *Learning for Leadership: Interpersonal and Intergroup Relations*. London: Tavistock.

Scharff, J. S. (1989). *Foundations of Object Relations Family Therapy*. New York: Jason Aronson.

Schwartz, H. S. (1990). *Narcissistic Process and Corporate Decay: The Theory of the Organizational Ideal*. New York: New York University Press.

Selznick, P. (1957) *Leadership in Administration: A Sociological Interpretation*. Berkeley, CA: University of California Press.

Semrad, E. V. (1969). *Teaching Psychotherapy of Psychotic Patients: Supervision of Beginning Residents in the 'Clinical Approach'*. New York: Grune & Stratton.

Shapiro, E. R. (1978a). Research on family dynamics: Clinical implications for the family of the borderline adolescent. *Adolescent Psychiatry, 6*: 360–376.

Shapiro, E. R. (1978b). The psychodynamics and developmental psychology of the borderline patient: A review of the literature. *American Journal of Psychiatry, 135*: 1305–1315.

Shapiro, E. R. (1982a). On curiosity: Intrapsychic and interpersonal boundary formation in family life. *International Journal of Family Psychiatry, 3*: 69–89.

Shapiro, E. R. (1982b). The holding environment and family therapy with acting out adolescents. *International Journal of Psychoanalytic Psychotherapy, 9*: 209–226.

Shapiro, E. R. (1985). Unconscious process in an organization: A serendipitous investigation. In: A. D. Coleman & M. H. Geller (Eds.), *Group Relations Reader II*. Washington, DC: A. K. Rice Institute.

Shapiro, E. R. (1987). Interpreting irrationality. In: J. Krantz (Ed.), *Irrationality in Social and Organizational Life* (pp. 1–9). Washington, DC: A. K. Rice Institute.

Shapiro, E. R. (Ed.) (1997a). *The Inner World in the Outer World: Psychoanalytic Perspectives*. New Haven, CT: Yale University Press.

Shapiro, E. R. (1997b). The boundaries are shifting: renegotiating the therapeutic frame In: E. R. Shapiro (Ed.), *The Inner World in the Outer World: Psychoanalytic Perspectives*. New Haven, CT: Yale University Press.

Shapiro, E. R. (2000a). The individual in context. In: J. J. Shay & J. Wheelis (Eds.), *Odysseys in Psychotherapy*. New York: Irvington.

Shapiro, E. R. (2000b). American voters: Optimistic and disenchanted. *American Psychoanalyst, 34*: 14.

Shapiro, E. R. (2001a). The effect of social changes on the doctor–patient relationship. *Organisational and Social Dynamics, 2*: 1–11.

Shapiro, E. R. (2001b). Institutional learning as chief executive. In: L. Gould, L. Stapley, & M. Stein, (Eds.), *The Systems Psychodynamics of Organizations: Integrating the Group Relations Approach, Psychoanalytic and Open Systems Theory*. New York: Karnac.

Shapiro, E. R. (2001c). The changing role of the CEO. *Organisational and Social Dynamics, 1*(1): 130–142.

Shapiro, E. R. (2003). The maturation of American identity: A study of the elections of 1996 and 2000 and the war against terrorism. *Organisational and Social Dynamics, 3*: 121–133.

Shapiro, E. R. (2004). Task: A transcendent notion. In: M. Percey (Ed.), *The Character of Wisdom: Essays in Honor of A. W. Carr*. London: Ashgate.

Shapiro, E. R. (2005). Joining a group's task: The discovery of hope and respect. *International Journal of Group Psychotherapy, 55*(2): 211–225.

Shapiro, E. R. (2009). Examined living: A psychodynamic treatment system. *Journal of the American Academy of Psychoanalysis and Dynamic Psychotherapy, 37*(4): 679–694.

Shapiro, E. R. (2012). Management versus interpretation: Teaching residents to listen. *Journal of Nervous and Mental Disease, 203*: 204–207.

Shapiro, E. R. (2013). Derailment in organizational development: Consultations to the Austen Riggs Center. *Organisational and Social Dynamics, 13*(1): 41–54.

Shapiro, E. R. (2016). Learning from the director's role: Leadership and irrationality. *Organisational and Social Dynamics, 16*(2): 255–270.

Shapiro, E. R. (2019). Wesley Carr, religious institutions, and institutional integrity. *Organisational and Social Dynamics, 19*(1): 103–111.

Shapiro, E. R., & Carr, A. W. (1987). Disguised countertransference in institutions. *Psychiatry, 50*: 72–82.

Shapiro, E. R., & Carr, A. W. (1991). *Lost in Familiar Places: Creating New Connections Between the Individual and Society*. New Haven, CT: Yale University Press.

Shapiro, E. R., & Carr, A. W. (2006). These people were some kind of solution: Can society in any sense be understood? *Organisational and Social Dynamics, 6*(2): 241–257.

Shapiro, E. R., & Carr, A. W. (2012). An introduction to Tavistock style group relations conference learning. *Organisational and Social Dynamics, 12*(1): 70–80.

Shapiro, E. R., & Freedman, J. (1987). Family dynamics of adolescent suicide. *Adolescent Psychiatry, 14*: 191–207.

Shapiro, E. R., & Fromm, M. (1999). Erik Erikson's clinical theory. In: B. Sadock & H. Kaplan (Eds.), *Comprehensive Textbook of Psychiatry*. Baltimore, MD: Lippincott, Williams & Wilkins.

Shapiro, E. R., & Kolb, J. E. (1979). Engaging the family of the hospitalized adolescent: The multiple family meeting. *Adolescent Psychiatry, 7*: 322–342.

Shapiro, E. R., & Plakun, E. M. (2009). Residential psychotherapeutic treatment: An intensive psychodynamic approach for patients with treatment-resistant disorders. In: S. Sharfstein (Ed.), *Textbook of Hospital Psychiatry*. Arlington, VA: American Psychiatric Publishing.

Shapiro, E. R., Shapiro, R. L., Zinner, J., & Berkowitz, D. A. (1977). The borderline ego and the working alliance: Indications for individual and family treatment in adolescence. *International Journal of Psychoanalysis, 58*: 77–87.

Shapiro, E. R., Zinner, J., Shapiro, R. L., & Berkowitz, D. A. (1975). The influence of family experience on borderline personality development. *International Review of Psycho-Analysis, 2*: 399–411.

Shapiro, R. L. (1966). Identity and ego autonomy in adolescence. In: J. Massennan (Ed.), *Science and Psychoanalysis*, New York: Grune & Stratton.

Shapiro, R. L., & Zinner, J. (1976). Family organization and adolescent development. In: E. J. Miller (Ed.), *Task and Organization*. London: Wiley.

Simon, B. (1996). Can there be a psychoanalyst without a political analysis? In C. Strozier (Ed.), *Genocide, War and Human Survival*. New York: Rowman & Littlefield.

Simon, H. A. (1997). *Administrative Behavior: A Study of Decision-Making Processes in Administrative Organizations*. New York: Free Press.

Singer, D., & Shapiro, E. R. (1988). Discovering the links between early family roles and current organizational roles: A loved and feared task (unpublished manuscript).

Singer, T. (Ed.) (1999). *The Vision Thing: Myth, Politics and Psyche in the World*. London: Routledge.

Stacey, R. D. (1992). *Managing the Unknowable: Strategic Boundaries between Order and Chaos in Organizations*. San Francisco, CA: Jossey-Bass.

Stacey, R. D. (1996). *Complexity and Creativity in Organizations*. San Francisco, CA: Berrett-Koehler.

Sullivan, H. S. (1953). *The Interpersonal Theory of Psychiatry*. New York: W. W. Norton.

Trist, E. L., & Sofer, C. (1959). *Exploration in Group Relations*. Leicester, UK: Leicester University Press.

Vaill, P. (1989). *Managing as a Performing Art*. San Francisco, CA: Jossey-Bass.

Volkan, V. (1998). *Bloodlines: From Ethnic Pride to Ethnic Terrorism*. New York: Basic Books.

Volkan, V. (2006a). *Killing in the Name of Identity: A Study of Bloody Conflicts*. Durham, NC: Pitchstone.

Volkan, V. (2006b). *Slobodan Milošević and the Reactivation of the Serbian Chosen Trauma*. New York: Clio.

Volkan, V., Akhtar, S., Dom, R., Kafka, J., Kernberg, O., Olsson, P., Rogers, R., & Shanfield, S. (1998). Psychodynamics of leaders and decision-making, *Mind and Human Interaction, 9*: 130–181.

Wells, L. J. (1995). The group-as-a-whole: A systemic socioanalytic perspective on interpersonal and group relations. In: J. Gillette & M. McCollom (Eds.), *Groups in Context: A New Perspective on Group Dynamics*. Reading, MA: Addison-Wesley.

Winnicott, D. W. (1960). The theory of the parent–infant relationship. In: *The Maturational Processes and the Facilitating Environment*. New York: International Universities Press, 1965.

Winnicott, D. W. (1963). Psychiatric disorders in terms of infantile maturational process. In: *The Maturational Processes and the Facilitating Environment*. New York: International Universities Press.

Zaleznick, A. (1989). *The Managerial Mystique: Restoring Leadership in Business*. New York: Harper & Row.

Zinner, J., & Shapiro, E. R. (1975). Splitting in the families of borderline adolescents. In: J. Mack (Ed.), *Borderline Slates in Psychiatry*. New York: Grune & Stratton.

Zinner, J., & Shapiro, R. L. (1972). Projective identification as a mode of perception and behavior in families of adolescents. *International Journal of Psycho-Analysis, 53*: 523–530.

Zinner, J., & Shapiro, R. L. (1974). The family as a single psychic entity: Implications for acting out in adolescents. *International Review of Psycho-Analysis, I*: 179–186.

Index

active citizenship, 17
adult role, constricted, 151 *see also* citizenship as development
AKRI *see* A. K. Rice Institute
A. K. Rice Institute (AKRI), 60, 70
American identity, 135
    America's outer boundaries, 135
    discussion, 145–146
    ethnic identifications, 138
    identity, 136–140
    integrity, 143
    Obama and Trump, 143–145
    presidential election of, 135
    split national identity, 135
    terrorist attacks of September 11, 141–143
    unaffiliated voters, 137
    white majority and election, 140–141
Annual Institute, 37, 40–41, 43–44
Armstrong, D., 114
attribution, 20

Austen Riggs Center, xxiii–xxiv, 4–5, 75–77, 81–83, 90, 94, 131, *see also* citizenship laboratory; mission; self-reflective organization development
    clinical mission of, 117
    consultations, 111
    derailment in mission of, 109
    developing identity, 93
    displacement of transference feelings, 103
    Friends Organization, 93
    mission, 94, 107
    nursing staff members, 117
    patients and relationships, 101
    Resource Management Committee, 91

Barber, B., 54
Bass, B. M., 50, 51, 53
belief, power of, 4–5
Bennis, W., 50

Bion, W. R., 20, 62, 65
Boguslaw, R., 51, 57
boundaries
 and authority, 79–80
 and Austen Riggs, 92
 of groups, 3, 5, 12, 39, 62–63, 67, 124–125
 organizational, 50–51, 54, 56, 71, 104, 110
 of nations, 58, 135–136 *see also* American identity
bounded entities, 157–158, 163–164
Buckup, S., 160

Carr, A. W., 5, 24, 27, 29, 37, 50, 52, 54, 57, 60, 61, 67, 69, 70, 71, 101, 114, 123, 124
Center for National Policy, 137
CEO *see also* leadership role
 discipline, 52
 mission statements, 56–57
 role of, 50, 52, 54
character change, 94
Chestnut Lodge, 86
chosen glories, 158
chosen traumas, 158
citizenship, 3
citizenship as development, 147
 constricted adult role, 151
 discovering bridging group, 155
 ethnic stereotyping, 147–148
 facing conflict with another person, 154–155
 joining polarized subgroup, 148
 membership, 149
 regression, 150
 roles and groups, 149–155
 taking up citizen role, 153–154
citizenship laboratory, 97
 community, 97–98, 101, 105
 contained environment and interpersonal learning, 98
 displacement of transference feelings, 103
 examined living, 97
 interpretive work and careful management, 105

 patients, 98–100
 problematic family and relationships, 97
 resisting caregivers, 100
 society, 107
 system management, 104–107
 taking charge, 100–104
 treatment-resistant psychiatric disorders, 98
Community Outreach Program, 92
constricted adult role, 151 *see also* citizenship as development
containment and communication, 11
 active citizenship, 17
 blaming the system, 17–18
 boundary between group, 12
 communication across organizations, 15–17
 consequences of failed containment, 12–14
 developmental vulnerabilities, 13
 development of irrational role, 13–14
 family containment, 12
 holding environment, 11–12
  failure in early childhood, 13–14
 irrational role creation, 13
 parental anxiety, 13
 parental love, 14
 pathological certainty, 12–13
 shared family regression, 13
 symptom bearer as messenger, 15–17
countertransference, 61, 101 *see also* transference

Democratic party, 109, 135–136, 139
development and family system, 13
distributed leadership, 53 *see also* leadership role

Elmendorf, D., 17, 105, 152
entrepreneurial leaders, 51 *see also* leadership role
Erikson, E. H., 50, 136
 identity formation, 136
 integrity, 143

Erikson Institute, 95, 112
Erlich, S., 148
ethnic stereotyping, 147–148
examined living, 90, 97

family
    containment, 12, see also
        containment and
        communication
    developmental task, 21
    holding environment, 30
    as an organization, 1, 3, 14, 32
    roles, 22, 24, 97, 100, 153, 157
    shared regression, 13
    symptom bearer, 15
Ferguson, N., 146
Fraher, A. L., 75, 114
Freud, S., 95
Fromm, M. G., 112, 132, 136, 143

Gilmore, T., 50, 51, 52
Gould, L., 114
group behavior, 21–22
group entities, 50
group relations conference, 59
    see also group relations and
        leadership
    ability to recognize group
        functioning, 62
    components of learning, 62
    conference as whole, 64
    determined focus on group and
        developing institution, 66–67
    group dynamics, 64–66
    holding and containment, 62–63
    individual member, 64
    moment within event, 64
    primary task, 69
    projective identification, 61
    psychoanalytic concepts, 61
    shared unconscious assumptions, 65–66
    specific events, 64
    specific group contexts, 63
    transference and
        countertransference, 61
    unconscious functioning, 61

group relations and leadership, 69 see
    also group relations conference
    conference administration, 72
    conference anxiety, 74–75
    directing Austen Riggs, 75–77
    directing conferences, 70–75
    institutional leaders, 71
    leader's vulnerability and
        dependency, 79
    mutual vulnerability of the
        authority boundary, 79
    returning to conferences, 77–80
    self-reflective organization and
        conference dynamics, 73
    treatment-resistant psychiatric
        patients, 75
    vulnerability of authorization, 79

Havel, V., 10
Havens, L., 62
Heifetz, R. A., 50, 51, 52, 53
Hendry, J., 50
Hirschhorn, L., 50, 51, 52, 114
holding environment, 11–12 see
    also containment and
    communication
    failure of, 13–14
    family, 12
humanity at intergroup learning, 159–160

identity, 136–140
    in context, 50
individual
    boundary, 3
    psychotherapy, 84
Institute Leader, 37–38 see also role, taking up
institutional
    leaders, 71
    missions, 56, 157
institutions, 55, 107, 109
    approaching society through, 123
    differing institutional contexts, 129–131
    discussion, 133
    interpretations, 129–131

interpreting society from linked
    institutions, 131–133
regression, 124
religious, 124–125
response to society's needs, 124–129
traditional to flexible structure, 111
ultimate boundaries, 125
working across institutional
    boundaries, 129–131
institutions-in-the-mind, 155
integrity, 143
internal experience, 29 *see also*
    interpretive stance
    fundamental aspect of, 29–30
    relatedness, 30, 164
    relationship, 30, 164
internal organizational structure, 53
interpretation, 19
interpretive stance, 33–35
    features, 27
    individual experience, 28–29
    using internal experience, 29–31
    negotiating interpretations and
        discerning relevant context,
        31–33
    organization's task, 32–33
irrational role creation, 5, 12–13, 30, 98,
    105, 107

Jaques, E., 53
Jewson, D., 58
Johnson, G., 50
joining a group, 3
    compelled for responsible citizen, 8
    discovering shared institutional
        task, 5–8
    taking up leadership role, 4–5

Kanter, R. M., 50, 54
Kelly, J., 50, 52
Kernberg, O., xix, 50, 52, 54
Khaleelee, O., 123, 152
Klein, E. B., 50, 51
Klein, M., xix, 61
Krantz, J., 51, 54

Laurie, D., 51, 52, 53
Lawrence, G., 50
leaders, 49
    types of, 51
leadership role, 49
    becoming part of organized
        group, 50
    in contemporary organizational
        life, 58
    contemporary society challenges, 58
    discovering bridging group, 155
    distributed leadership, 53
    entrepreneurial leaders, 51
    grappling with systems pressures, 49
    identity in context, 50
    internalized social structures, 52
    irrationality and group dynamics, 49
    leader as person, 51–53
    leadership of changing
        organizations, 53–55
    organization and institution, 55–58
    requirements, 51, 69, 147
    role of CEO, 50, 54
    use of self-reflective humor, 54–55
limited resources, 91
Lofgren, D. P., 75

managed-care companies, 94
membership, 149 *see also* citizenship as
    development
Menzies, I. E. P., 53
Miller, E. J., 20, 52, 53, 54, 58, 60,
    123, 114
Mintz, D., 112
mission, 110–111
    collegial collaboration, 112
    corporate mentality, 112
    data of systems psychodynamics, 114
    dependency and autonomy, 109,
        115–118
    derailment and recalibration of, 109
    discussion, 118–119
    external consultation, 112
    internal organizational structure,
        111–115

learning on behalf of society, 119
meetings and languages, 112–113
pairing dynamic, 114
Modell, A. H., 12, 104, 110
mother–baby pair, 163
Muller, J. P., 112
multicellular learning system, 157
multiple memberships, 147, 149,
    152–154, 157

Obama, B., 137, 143–144 *see also*
    American identity
Obholzer, A., 114
open systems, 53, 104, 110
organizational dynamics, 19
    attribution, 20
    family role and organizational role,
        22–24
    individual experience, 19–20
    interpretation, 19
    negative authorization, 24
    roles and task, 24–26
    primary task, 20
    shared unconscious assumptions in
        groups, 21
    task, 20–21
    unconscious group behavior, 21–22
organizations *see also* leadership role;
    mission
    communication across, 15–17
    conflicts between profit and social
        responsibility, 58
    experiences and formulations, 119
    and institutions, 55–58
    institutional missions, 56
    internal structure, 53
    leadership of changing, 53–55
    membership, 149
    primary task, 110
    task of, 32–33

Palmer, B., 62
para-therapeutic groups, 38
parental love, 14
Parish, M., 17, 63, 72, 105, 152

pathological certainty, 12–13, 79
peer group, 3
Pelton, W. J., 50, 51, 57
Perry, C. J., 112
Plakun, E. M., 75, 112
polarized subgroup, joining, 148
power of belief, 4–5
problematic family and relationships, 97
projective identification, 61, 100–101,
    107, 152

regression, 124, 150
    regressive phenomenon, 159
    and religion, 125
    shared family, 13
relatedness, 30, 164
relationship, 30, 164
    problematic family and, 97
religion, 124–125, 127–128
religious institutions, 124–125 *see also*
    institutions
    funeral of Diana, 125–129
    rituals, 125
    societal influence, 125
Republican party, 109, 135–136, 139,
    141–142
Rice, A. K., 58, 60, 114
Rioch, M., 77
rituals, 125
Roberts, V. Z., 114
role, taking up, 4–5, 37
    Annual Institute, 37
    authority dilemmas and
        collaborative data, 43
    demonstration interview with
        family, 39
    discussion, 44–45
    Institute Leader, 37–38
    integrating didactic material and
        group experience, 40
    interpretive hypothesis, 40
    looking for connections to
        experience, 42
    negotiated interpretation, 44
    para-therapeutic groups, 38

Sackmann, S., 51, 57
Scharff, J. S., 21
Schwartz, H. S., 50
self-reflective organization
　　development, 81
　　examined living, 90
　　focusing on citizenship, 95
　　homogenization of staff, 88
　　individual psychotherapy, 84
　　institutional mission, 83
　　joining outside world and clarifying mission, 92–95
　　learning about institution, 83–84
　　limited resources, 91
　　mission, 94
　　power vs. authority, 84
　　principles, 81–82
　　renegotiating mission, 85
　　Riggs' identity, 93
　　shaping management structures, 86–89
　　symbolic communication from staff, 85–86
　　treatment resistant, 93
　　unique institutional values, 89–92
Selznick, P., 56
Semrad, E. V., vi, xii
Shapiro, E. R., 5, 12, 22, 24, 27, 29, 37, 50, 51, 52, 54, 57, 60, 61, 67, 69, 71, 75, 77, 81, 90, 101, 109, 110, 114, 124, 128, 136, 137, 143, 148
Shapiro, R. L., 21, 61
shared family regression, 13
shared unconscious assumptions in groups, 21 *see also* organizational dynamics
Simon, B., 95
Simon, H. A., 50, 58
Singer, D., 22
Singer, T., 145
society, 107, 123
　　being member of, 163
　　chosen glories, 158
　　chosen traumas, 158
　　humanity at intergroup learning, 159–160

institutional missions, 157
institutions and, 123
　　as multicellular learning system, 157–161
　　regressive phenomenon, 159
　　subgroupings, 150
Sofer, C., 60
split national identity, 135 *see also* American identity
Stacey, R. D., 50, 53, 57
Stein, M., 54, 58
Sullivan, H. S., 62
symptom change, 94
systems *see also* group relations conference
　　dynamics, 49
　　psychodynamics, 59

task, 20–22 *see also* organizational dynamics
Tillman, J. G., 112
transference, 61, 101, 103 *see also* countertransference
treatment resistance, 93, 98
　　psychiatric disorders, 98
　　psychiatric patients, 75
Trist, E. L., 60
Trump, D., 137, 143, 144–145, 151 *see also* American identity

unaffiliated voters, 137
unconscious *see also* organizational dynamics
　　functioning, 61
　　group behavior, 21–22

Vaill, P., 50, 52
Volkan, V., 50, 52, 158
voters, unaffiliated, 137

Wells, L. J., 114
Winnicott, D. W., 11, 163

Zaleznick, A., 50
Zheutlin, B., 112
Zinner, J., 21, 61

Made in United States
North Haven, CT
13 February 2022